Breaking Away From the Textbook

Creative Ways to Teach World History

Ron H. Pahl

Volume 1
Prehistory to 1600

Rowman & Littlefield Education
Lanham • Boulder • New York • Toronto • Plymouth, UK
2002

This title was originally published by ScarecrowEducation.
First Rowman & Littlefield Education edition 2006.

Published in the United States of America
by Rowman & Littlefield Education
A Division of Rowman & Littlefield Publishers, Inc.
A wholly owned subsidiary of The Rowman & Littlefield Publishing Group, Inc.
4501 Forbes Boulevard, Suite 200, Lanham, Maryland 20706
www.rowmaneducation.com

Estover Road
Plymouth PL6 7PY
United Kingdom

British Library Cataloguing in Publication Information Available

Library of Congress Cataloging-in-Publication Data
Pahl, Ron H., 1943-
    Breaking away from the textbook : creative ways to teach world history /
    Ron H. Pahl.
        p. cm. – (A Scarecrow education book)
    Includes bibliography.
    Contents: v. 1. Prehistory to 1600 – v. 2. The enlightenment through the
    twentieth century.
    ISBN 0-8108-3759-5 (alk. paper)
        1. History–Study and teaching. I. Title.
    D16.2 .P24 2002   2001020970
    907'.1–dc21
v. 2 ISBN 0-8108-3760-9
set ISBN 0-8108-3761-7

⊖™ The paper used in this publication meets the minimum requirements of
American National Standard for Information Sciences—Permanence of
Paper for Printed Library Materials, ANSI/NISO Z39.48-1992.
Manufactured in the United States of America.

Contents

List of Illustrations

Acknowledgments

This work could not have been accomplished without the unwavering support and commitment of my wife, Jarvis, and my young adult children, Mothusi and Leloba. The others whose suggestions greatly improved the quality of *Creative Ways to Teach World History* are Dick and Judy Kraft, Nelson and JoAnne Woodard, Bill Lacey, John Bovberg, and Ron Evans. Also not to be forgotten are the many teachers and student teachers who tested, commented on, and corrected items in the Thematic Learning Pacs in these volumes.

When was the last time you lugged an 800-page textbook around with you all day? Could you not help but be irritated at the book, even without cracking the cover? Now open this giant tome (tomb?) of strange names and dates, which have no apparent meaning to anyone today. Imagine sitting through a class based on this textbook. The thought is downright frightening. No wonder students often list world history as their *least* favorite subject in school. But now there is hope! Wilma Cordero and Shelly Kintisch published a delightful little book a few years back entitled *Breaking Away from the Textbook: A Creative Approach to Teaching American History* for Technomic. Cordero and Kintisch, in a delightful romp through American history, present teachers with a ton of ideas on how to teach history without getting bogged down in all the names, dates, and drudgery of a typical history textbook. Teaching American history can now be exciting for the student and the teacher: How about twenty-nine ideas on how to teach about the Old West or thirty-two ideas for projects to teach about the 1960s?

Breaking Away from the Textbook: Creative Ways to Teach World History applies the same ideas to teaching as Cordero and Kintisch did, but for world history. From the size of this volume, you can tell it is not a comprehensive world history guide, nor is it a text heavy into theory. Instead, this book focuses on the following:

- A wide variety of active teaching ideas for world history
- A large number of ideas on how to get students excited about world history

- How-to-do-it brainstorms for teachers who know they need help
- Creative ways to have students grapple with the major problems and issues humanity has faced throughout history
- Innovative ways to help students see the relevance of major people, events, and ideas of the past to our lives today

Simply put, the purpose of the book is to make world history fun. This book, however, is not for everyone. Those who should not use the book are the following:

- Teachers who enjoy boring their students with endless lectures
- Teachers who believe that their students must memorize every name and date in their textbook
- Teachers who demand a quiet classroom with students reading their textbook, and answering the questions at the end of the unit

A word of caution, however: Reading the textbook is important. The active learning strategies presented in this book are not meant to discourage reading. Rather, these strategies are designed to get students turned on to the ideas and problems humans have faced throughout history. Students who are interested in the subject are going to want to read the text and other sources of history. These turned-on students are going to want to read more, write more, and think more about how to solve the major problems we have faced throughout history. These are the kind of students we want to be the decision makers of the future.

In these opening years of the twenty-first century, all of us are facing information overload. The amount of information in the world is doubling every year. The need is not for more memorization of trivial facts from the past, but rather the development of skills in the analysis of this information in order to decipher what is important in making present and future decisions. The active learning strategies presented in this book—through Thematic Lesson Pacs—are designed to promote and develop skills that can focus on, and differentiate between, essential and nonessential information. Such skills will be essential in our new century as new information and ideas continue to rapidly expand.

As a way of introduction, some of the major active learning strategies presented in each Thematic Learning Pac (TLP) are as follows:

Quick Writes   Diary Entries
Role Plays   Poet Corners
Viewpoints   Art Marts
Photo Analysis   Songs and Rap Fests
Map Attacks   Front Page Newspapers
Concept Webbing   Travel Brochures
Venn Diagrams   Dioramas and Models
T Charts   "You Were There" Interviews
Time Lines   Slogans and Graffiti
Pair Shares   Bumper Stickers
Quick Skits   Quick Calcs
What If?   History Chains
Spin Doctors   Pros and Cons
Counter Spins   Research Projects
Time Travelers   Futurists
Talk Show Hosts   Action Research
Poster Power   Opinion Polls

It is the sincere desire of this author to have students excited about world history. This book is far from complete when considering all of the possible topics to cover in world history. It is the wish of the author, however, that teachers will use this book as a starting point for their own creativity. Apply the teaching ideas from this book to other topics in history. History does not have to be an endless list of dead men entombed between the covers of a textbook. Use this book as a starting point to build student enthusiasm for world history. Such excitement can then have an amazing ripple effect. Teachers become more interested in teaching. Schools become more exciting places to be. More learning takes place, and suddenly the world is becoming a better place. It can be done.

Ron H. Pahl
California State University, Fullerton

Introduction: History—What, Why, and How?

What Is History?

The original meaning of the word "history" in classic Greek was "inquiry" (Collingwood 1956). More recently, the word has taken the meaning "to inquire about the past."

Why History?

Why do people "inquire about the past?" There are many reasons. Some people just want to know where they came from. Others want to look backward to find ancestors they can brag about to their neighbors. Some folks just do not like the present and want to complain that things just aren't like what they used to be in the good old days. Socrates (469–399 B.C.E.) in ancient Greece was one of these. He made the following complaint:

> Children now love luxury. They have bad manners and contempt for authority. They show disrespect for their elders and love chatter in place of exercise. They no longer rise when their elders enter the room. They contradict their parents, chatter before company, gobble up dainties at the table, and tyrannize their teachers.

History has a much more important purpose. Humans throughout history have faced a variety of problems—some of which have never been solved. The result is that we still face many of these same problems and countless new ones as we move into the twenty-first century. As participating citizens of the world, we need to examine the records of the past to understand how humans in other times grappled with their problems—where they succeeded and where they failed. From this analysis, we can build on the experience of the past and better prepare ourselves for the future.

How Should We Study World History?

Most world history books are structured chronologically region by region (see appendix B for traditional chronological and regional table of contents of *Breaking Away*). A result of this structure is that students often miss the truly global impact of many new ideas and changes in history, and the different ways humans around the world reacted to these changes. The activities in this book are organized in chronological units around fourteen global themes in history in order to grasp the monumental impact different people, events, and ideas have had on the world as a whole. These fourteen global themes will form the fundamental structure for each unit in the book. The themes—plus a short description—are as follows:

THEMATIC LESSON PACS (TLP)

1. Historical Time Line

In the physical universe, there may be no such thing as time, neither a beginning nor an ending (Hawking 1990). If we follow Hawking and the other quantum physics folks, the concept of time is a human invention. We humans seem to want beginnings and endings to our human story. Following this human convention of time, this book will use a simple B.C.E./C.E. (Before the Current Era/Current Era) dating pattern based on the birth of Jesus in developing a historical time line. As we pass into the twenty-first century, however, we must realize that this time scale is relative. Different cultures and religions have different time lines. Many of the dates used in this book are also approximations and may contain inaccuracies in the B.C.E./C.E. time line we have chosen to use in this book.

Another interesting question is the shape of history. Is it circular and constantly repeating itself, as the Greeks saw it? Does history move in a straight line toward a distant goal, such as the Christian concept of salvation envisioned by St. Augustine or the Marxist idea of utopia? Does it move in wavy lines with high and low periods? Or does it parallel modern quantum physics and move chaotically with repeating iterations, but also constantly changing at the same time?

2. Separating Fact from Myth and Propaganda

A major problem in history is the determination of what is fact and what is fiction. The cynic who said, "History is written by the winners" is often correct. We, as inquiring historians, must be aware of the point of view taken by an author and be able to distinguish blatant propaganda and deliberate misinformation from accurate information. A common problem occurs when major people of history begin to take on superhuman characteristics. This process of myth making has taken place throughout history, many times innocently, as stories are repeated around the campfire. Often, however, this myth-making process becomes deliberate when cultures invent their heroes and even their gods. This process of myth making often takes regular forms or archetypes that we can look for in all cultures throughout history (Pearson 1989):

- The Warrior who can conquer any foe—Alexander the Great
- The Martyr who sacrifices his life for a cause—Socrates
- The Magician who has the power to defy nature—Moses
- The Wanderer who single-handedly discovers new worlds—Columbus
- The Villain whose evil deeds darken even the sun—Attila the Hun

When people in history begin to take on the characteristics of these mythological archetypes, we need to be cautious about accepting this information as fact. Such mythological characters may be the central focus of our comic-book heroes and antiheroes, but if we are not careful, they are treated as the factual characters of our history books. Determining the facts of history from centuries of mythology is obviously a difficult task, but one which we must undertake.

3. Location and Movement

Where an item or idea comes from is critical in its historical development; equally important is how it spreads or does not spread across the world. For example, citrus fruit comes from Persia. If citrus fruit came originally from Australia, it would likely have remained as a novel local food and not spread rapidly across the world until modern times. Persia, on the other hand, had trade routes both east to China and west to Europe at a very early date, and citrus seeds were easily carried along these routes to other corners of the world. The location and dissemination of historical items are therefore critical in understanding the successes and failures of individuals and even whole empires.

4. Politics and Leadership

Much of current textbook history focuses on the great deeds of heroic individuals and countries (see mythology above). To understand what happened in history, however, we must look behind the individual or country. What makes a leader or a country successful or a failure? What kind of political system was used to achieve success? What were its weaknesses and what were its strengths? Is this a type of system we will want to use in the twenty-first century?

5. Social and Economic Life

Was life better in the good old days? Or not? What social and economic features of past societies should we retain for the future, and which features should we leave in the history books? In eras of rapid change such as our own, we need to carefully review our social and economic lifestyles, decide what we want and do not want, and then deliberately work toward creating a better life for all of us.

6. Religious Thought

Who is God? How have different people throughout history viewed God? Why is religious worship so different across the world? Some of the most powerful thinking of humankind has been devoted to religious thought. Some of the most savage acts in history have also been done in the name of religion. The activities presented in this book are designed to further a wider understanding and respect between all our common human religious beliefs.

7. Conquest and Warfare

Conquests and warfare, at times, seem endemic to humanity. Traditional history books tend to spend a great deal of time fighting battles. The activities in this book are designed to go beyond these individual battles and examine the causes, repercussions, and possible diplomatic alternatives of war. The aim of these activities is to present students with options beyond war to draw from when they are faced with the critical decision of war or peace in the future.

8. Tragedy and Disaster

History is full of both human-made tragedies and natural disasters. Many of these disasters, such as the Black Death of 1331 C.E., drastically changed the course of history. The activities in this book will bring the experience of the massive impact of these disasters home to the students. How can individuals, families, and nations cope with such disasters? Can students in class obtain the skills and the foresight to reduce the agony or avoid such tragedies and disasters in the future?

9. Exploration and Discovery

Many of the high points of history are of human exploration and discovery. Centuries can go by without much change in human knowledge or understanding. Suddenly the conditions during a particular era are right and humans begin to explore new lands and make discoveries that improve their lives. The seemingly simple discovery that seeds from grain could be stored and planted each year was one of the major discoveries of humankind. Why do some societies explore widely and make new discoveries and others do very little? What impact do new discoveries have on the human condition? What new discoveries can we expect in the future?

10. Invention and Revolution

The explorers in history get all the glory. Inventors, however, often make as many or more important changes, but we rarely ever know their names. New ideas also rarely happen in isolation. The activities in this book examine the conditions leading to several major historical inventions (such as the transistor in 1947), the impact of these inventions, and the social and economic revolutions that often follow their introduction.

11. Art and Creative Thought

The joy and agony of human existence is often expressed in art, poetry, music, and other forms of creative thought. From the cave paintings of

Lascaux (circa 10,000 B.C.E.) to the singing of "Hard Day's Night" by the Beatles (1964), human creative expression is reflective of each historical era. The activities in this book examine such creative efforts of each era to better understand the joy and agony of what it means to be human.

12. Successes and Failures of an Era

At the conclusion of each era, it is important for inquiring historians to reflect on the successes and failures of the era. What did humanity learn about itself during each period?

13. Major Historical Problems

Kenneth Boulding (1964) proposed that history should be studied through the major unresolved problems faced by humanity. Following Boulding, this book examines seven such problems throughout history:

1. The Problem of Justice: Tyranny is universally recognized as being wrong, but it continues unabated. More difficult for a nation is the delicate balance between individual liberty and equality for all (Mortimer Adler).
2. The Problem of War and Inhumanity: War and inhumanity toward other humans are universally recognized as evil, but war and inhumanity continue to thrive—and even prosper.
3. The Problem of Poverty: Despite the tremendous wealth and resources available, poverty remains a major global issue.
4. The Problem of Ecology: Human progress has been made, often to the detriment of the quality of human life and the natural environment.
5. The Problem of Ideology: Good ideas often become ritualized into ideology and important changes are rejected in the name of that ideology.
6. The Problem of Technology: Technological advances often take precedence over thoughtful leadership as a society blindly follows new innovations.
7. The Problem of Entropy: Humans have limited amounts of resources. When these resources are directed towards one goal, that action limits the number of resources that can be utilized

in other directions. A system—overcommitted to one direction—has a difficult time adapting to change. Irreversible decline sets in, followed by entropy, extinction, and replacement by another system.

14. Era Antecedents for the Future

At the conclusion of each era, major antecedents of the future will be identified and analyzed. The activities in *Breaking Away from the Textbook: Creative Ways to Teach World History* ask students to analyze the impact such inventions may have on the future. What do the antecedents of these inventions look like today? What will similar inventions look like in the future? At the conclusion of each era of time, students will role-play persons with five different viewpoints of the time period—from archconservative to radical progressive—to decide whether or not humankind is ready to advance to the next era. From each unit, students will discover that the door to the future can never be closed completely, and that we must always peek around the door to see what the next era has in store for us. Einstein said it wisely: "To make new discoveries and improve the human condition, we must go beyond current thinking."

The Thematic Organization of *Breaking Away*

Based on the thematic outline described above, the following units of *Breaking Away from the Textbook: Creative Ways to Teach World History* follow a general chronological development of the history of humankind:

Volume 1:
      Unit 1   Prehistory
      Unit 2   Ancient History
      Unit 3   Middle Ages
      Unit 4   Renaissance, Explorations, and Reformation

Volume 2:
      Unit 5   Enlightenment
      Unit 6   Nineteenth Century
      Unit 7   Twentieth Century

Each unit, in turn, has the following:

1. Introduction
2. Thematic Lesson Pacs for the unit, which follow the fourteen historical themes described above.
    1. Historical Time Line
    2. Separating Fact from Myth and Propaganda
    3. Location and Movement
    4. Politics and Leadership
    5. Social and Economic Life
    6. Religious Thought
    7. Conquest and Warfare
    8. Tragedy and Disaster
    9. Exploration and Discovery
    10. Invention and Revolution
    11. Art and Creative Thought
    12. Successes and Failure of an Era
    13. Major Historical Problems
    14. Era Antecedents for the Future

The core of *Breaking Away from the Textbook: Creative Ways to Teach World History* is the Thematic Lesson Pacs (TLP), arranged by each of the fourteen themes in each unit. Each TLP has a short selection of text and a variety of creative ways to study each theme, such as the following:

- Quick Write
- Map Attack
- Bumper Sticker
- Poster Power
- Spin Doctor
- Counter Spin
- Music Mart
- Quick Skit
- Poet's Corner
- ADV Historical Analysis (Advanced)

This thematic organization of *Breaking Away from the Textbook: Creative Ways to Teach World History* presents the teacher and the student with a great many interesting options to study history: Perhaps a study of myths and hero images across time following theme 2 for each era of history. Or perhaps a study of the major problems humankind has faced throughout history following theme 13 in each unit. Better yet, just wander through *Breaking Away* and pick out Thematic Lesson Pacs that look interesting and try them out in class. *Breaking Away* was designed as an enjoyable, challenging history cookbook.

Each Thematic Lesson Pac is numbered exactly by both unit and theme to easily and quickly identify each TLP. Three examples of this numbering system are as follows:

3.2.2 The P.R. Spin of Attila the Hun (circa 451 C.E.)
TLP 3.2.2. on Attila the Hun is located in
1. The 3rd unit—the Middle Ages
2. The 2nd theme on Mythology and Propaganda
3. The 2nd TLP on the theme of Mythology and Propaganda in the unit.

5.3.1 The Problem of Longitude
TLP 5.3.1 on Longitude is located in
1. The 5th unit—the Enlightenment
2. The 3rd theme on Location and Movement
3. The 1st TLP on the theme of Location and Movement in the unit.

7.11.3 Marxist Anarchy—Duck Soup!
TLP 7.11.3 on Marxist Anarchy (the Marx Brothers) is located in
1. The 7th unit—the Twentieth Century
2. The 11th theme on Art and Creative Thought
3. The 3rd TLP on the theme of Art and Creative Thought in the unit.

A quick perusal of *Breaking Away* will also verify that each Thematic Lesson Pac follows a fairly regular pattern. This pattern is no accident, but rather a subtle form of instructional assistance and utilization of multiple intelligences, which will be noticed when each TLP is used in class by the teacher.

1. Quick Writes are often the first activity in each TLP and form easy-to-use anticipatory sets to settle a new class down on a specific

writing assignment as the students come in the door of the classroom. This also enables the teacher to take care of classroom ad-
ministrative tasks while the students are writing. Each Quick Write
focuses on relating the specific historical theme or problem of the
TLP to each student's personal experience; sharing these experiences with the class as a whole can be an excellent entry point to
begin the actual lesson.

2. Concept Webs are also a great way to open a class and find out
   what students in the class know about a concept or phrase. They
   are very easy to do. Just place a word or phrase on the board. Circle it, and then ask students what they think when they see the
   word or phrase. Draw a line outward from the circle and write
   down each student response at the end of each line. The teacher
   should write down each student response whether right or wrong.
   The lesson following the Concept Web can clarify the word or
   phrase and naturally correct any misconceptions the students
   have about it.
3. Map Attacks, Art Marts, and Poster Powers all focus on developing students' spatial intelligence.
4. Quick Calcs focus on improving each student's mathematical-
   analytical intelligence.
5. Dramatizations and Quick Skits add to students' bodily kines-
   thetic, verbal-linguistic, and interpersonal intelligences.
6. Diary Entries improve each student's verbal-linguistic and intra-
   personal skills.
7. Historical Analyses (Advanced) add to each student's verbal-
   linguistic and mathematical-analytical skills.

And Don't Forget the Appendices:

Appendix F   Annotated Bibliography of all resources used in the compilation of *Breaking Away*

It is this educator's sincere wish that the active thematic organization of world history presented in *Breaking Away from the Textbook: Creative Ways to Teach World History* will stimulate an exciting, enjoyable classroom and will promote thoughtful decision making in tomorrow's adults.

Prehistory (4 Million B.C.E. to 3000 B.C.E.)

UNIT 1: TABLE OF CONTENTS

INTRODUCTION

The Prehistoric Era

Humans are certainly interesting animals. This chapter focuses on having students analyze the uniqueness of humans. Through these activities, students will experience the painfully slow development of early human prehistory—the first discoveries of fire, tools, religion, art, and the rudimentary problems of living together. There are triumphs in the discoveries of early humans, but there is also a great deal of pain, hardship, and lack of advancement. Why did it take so long for humans to develop simple things like knives, pots, and bread? The students must grapple with these very basic and fundamental problems of being humans.

THEMATIC LESSON PACS

1.1.0   HISTORICAL TIME LINE

1.1.1   Prehistoric History Time Line

• Name Plates: Photocopy six sets of the following ten names and items. Cut each name or item onto a strip of paper. Place the strips of

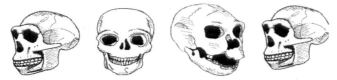

Illustration 1.1.1.   *Four Prehistoric Skulls*

paper carefully into separate envelopes for each team and label the envelopes "1.1.1 The Prehistoric History Time Line" for later use in class.

- Team Power: Break the class into six teams.
- The Envelope: Each team should be given an envelope containing the following random ten names from the prehistoric era:
  1. Discovery of agriculture and farming in the Middle East (9000 B.C.E.).
  2. Modern-looking *Homo antecessor* (circa 800,000 B.C.E.) lived in Spain and England.
  3. Earliest direct human ancestor *Homo ergaste* (2–1.5 million years B.C.E.) lived in Africa and used simple stone tools.
  4. Heavy-skulled *Homo Neanderthal* (circa 300,000 B.C.E.) lived in Europe.
  5. First use of metal tools made out of bronze (3000 B.C.E.) in the Middle East and Southeast Asia.
  6. First small villages of people (7,000 B.C.E.) in the Middle East.
  7. Magnetic pole reversal (740,000 B.C.E.).
  8. Near-relative *Homo erectus* (3–1 million years B.C.E.) lived in Africa and then Asia.
  9. Discovery of animal herding of reindeer in Europe (12,000 B.C.E.).
  10. Modern *Homo sapiens* (circa 100,000 B.C.E.) moved out of Africa into the Middle East, Asia, and Europe.
- Team Time Line: The first job of each team is to correctly order the ten names and artifacts according to time, with the oldest at the top and the most recent at the bottom. Each student should separately write the correct time line for the prehistoric names and artifacts on a personal sheet of paper for later reference.
- Team Look Up: Once every member of the team has the prehistoric time line written on a sheet of paper, each of the ten prehistoric names should be divided between members of the team to find out

the meaning of each name from the textbook. Once found, the meanings of each prehistoric name can be shared with the members of the team to write in each individual time line.

- Poster Power: On a large piece of paper, each team should construct its own time line for the prehistoric era using the ten names, with descriptions and illustrations, to demonstrate the meaning of each name. When finished, these can be presented to the class and displayed on the classroom wall.
- Music Mart: Each team should pick what they think is the most important name or event in the time line and then compose and present a short song or rap about the name or event. When finished, this can be presented to the class.
- Journal Entry: Have team members write a short journal entry speculating about what they now know about the development of humans during the prehistoric era—from the time line they developed—and possibly the most important things to happen during this era. When finished, students can first share their thoughts with their team and then with the class as a whole for general discussion about what they think are the most important things that happened during the era.

1.1.2   Prehistoric History Chain

A fun way to conduct an end-of-unit review for assessment is to create a class history chain. The steps to conduct a history chain are as follows:

1. The teacher should place each of the major names (without years attached) mentioned in the unit on an 8½"-×-11" sheet of paper, using a minimum of a 72-point typeface so everyone can read the name across the room. These names on paper should also be collected at the end of the lesson and stored in a folder for multiple use.
2. To begin the lesson, each student should stand and come to the front of the room and randomly be given one of the names. The students should then hold the names in front of them—facing outward—so that everybody in class can see the name.
3. The students should now make themselves into a prehistoric history chain by having the student with the oldest name, event, or thing at one far corner of the room and then placing themselves

in chronological order across the front of the room to the most recent name, event, or thing in another corner of the room. (Expect fun chaos as students can talk to each other and determine—by themselves—their own chronological order.)

4. Once the prehistoric history chain has been established, the teacher can review the chain by having the students identify their name, event, or thing and its relative place in the time line. (The teacher can expect to have more than a few corrections to make as each student describes the name and its time in history—but remember, this is an excellent and fun way to review.)

5. As a second step in the history chain, the teacher should group the students into teams of about six students each in order to have each team determine the most important name in their part of the chain for its impact on the world.

6. The teacher should then collect all the history chain name papers and save them to be used later. Students may then take their seats.

7. In a short journal entry, each student should then record what he or she thinks are the three most important things that happened in the era and then share them with the class to generate a full-class consensus on the meaning of the era.

1.2.0   SEPARATING FACT FROM MYTH AND PROPAGANDA

1.2.1   Human vs. Animal

In what ways are animals and humans similar? In what ways are humans and animals different from each other?

- T Chart: Using a T chart, make a list of at least five differences between animals and humans; for example, animals make noises to each other, but only humans can really talk to each other. Compare answers with everyone in class to make a large class T chart.

1.2.2   Early Human Homesite

Contrary to most stories and cartoons, most early humans likely did *not* live in caves, nor did they live in trees. We know they lived near water in order to drink and to catch the animals that came to drink. They knew how to make fire (since about one million B.C.E.). They knew how to make simple shelters out of branches and reeds. For the past several million years, early humans have made many of their heavy tools out of stone and their lighter tools out of wood. When it was cold, early humans certainly wore animal skins for protection, and lighter clothing when it was warm.

- Art Mart: Make an illustration of what you think an early human homesite would have looked like. Include things early humans might have had, such as a fire, clothes, a small hut, and stone tools.
- Bumper Sticker: Create a bumper sticker that you think early humans might wear on their animal skins—once they learned how to write.
- Diorama: Create a diorama or three-dimensional model of an early human site.
- ADV Research Project: Using your library or the Internet, pick one of the early humans or prehumans and find out more about what we know about them. When finished, report your findings to the class.

1.2.3   Neanderthal

Homo sapiens Neanderthalensis ("*Homo Neanderthal*") were big, heavyset people with large brow ridges who lived in Europe between 300,000 B.C.E. and the end of the last Ice Age, approximately 12,500 B.C.E. As modern *Homo sapiens*, *Homo Neanderthal* evidently descended from modern-looking *Homo antecessor* (circa 800,000 B.C.E.) who lived in Spain and England. Although heavy and tough looking, Neanderthals were sensitive, loved flowers, and buried their dead with honor. As with other early human beings, they also practiced cannibalism in times of starvation. We also know that *Homo Neanderthal* was similar to modern human beings, but they had different DNA sequences than humans and therefore did not intermarry, and were not ancestors of modern human *Homo sapiens* (Kunzig 1997).

- Quick Skit: Develop a short skit demonstrating what might have happened if a modern human met a Homo Neanderthal on the open plains near a stream of running water.
- Tear Jerker: Create a short, made-for-TV drama which depicts a heartbroken Neanderthal male who falls in love with a beautiful Homo sapiens female, but realizes that he will never be able to marry her because their DNA do not match.

- Counter Spin: Develop a late-developing news flash where the brothers of a young human female rescue her from a kidnap attempt by a heavy-set Neanderthal male.

1.3.0   LOCATION AND MOVEMENT

1.3.1   Early Human Drama

In a short dramatization, pretend that your class is a large family of early humans in Africa. Everyone is huddled around a large campfire (the middle of the classroom or outside in the grass).

A major debate is raging among the family members. Should the family leave Africa to live elsewhere in the world or not (circa 1 million B.C.E.)?

- Pros or Cons?: Pick a side of the argument.
- Defend It: Write an argument supporting whether to leave or not, and then stand up in front of the fire and present your argument to the family.
- Plenary Session: After everyone has presented their arguments, have the family vote whether to leave Africa or not, and present the reasons for their choice.

1.4.0   POLITICS AND LEADERSHIP

1.4.1   An Early Human Family Structure

The earliest humans most likely lived in small extended family units.

- Family Tree: Create a family tree of the family members and close friends who live with you.
- What If?: Imagine that all of you are early humans living together over 100,000 years ago.
- Task Master: Make a list of tasks for each family member and friend to assist in the survival of everyone. Remember, early humans at that time had little more than simple stone and wooden tools, and fires to keep warm and cook meat.
- Art Mart: Draw a picture of what you think your family might have looked like in 100,000 B.C.E.

1.4.2   How to Rule a Small Neolithic Village

Sometime after the end of the last Ice Age, circa 12,500 B.C.E., a smart young woman, gathering seeds to eat, noticed that dropped seeds—with a little water—grew into full plants after a few months. She had made one of the major discoveries in the world—the discovery of agriculture. Soon, humans in many different parts of the world began to drop wheat, sorghum, and rice seeds in the ground. Archaeologists called this period the *Neolithic, the New Stone Age*. People who grew their own grain to eat had to live in one area to take care of their crops, instead of being a nomadic people wandering around looking for food. These New Stone Age farmers began to make fine, small stone knives to harvest their wheat. They also became the first people to live in small agricultural villages. Around 7000 B.C.E., the first real political leaders in the world were the men and women who developed the first small agricultural villages during the Neolithic in the Middle East.

- Quick Write: In a short paragraph, give a description of what you think it would be like to live in one of the first small agricultural villages in the Middle East about 7000 B.C.E.
- Name Maker: In a team of four students from the same New Stone Age village, create a name for your village.
- Rule Maker #1: As the leaders of one of the first small villages in the world, what rules would your team of four create for the village?
- Rule Maker #2: How would your team create these rules?
- Rule Maker #3: Would your team involve others in making these rules? If so, how would you involve them?
- Plenary Session: Have each team share its ideas for ruling the village with the class and have the class determine which team made the best rules.
- ADV Historical Research: As an advanced project, search your school library and the Internet for information on how early Neolithic villages and small states were ruled. When finished, report your findings to the class.

1.5.0   SOCIAL AND ECONOMIC LIFE

1.5.1   Making Early Human Tools

Animals such as baboons will occasionally use tools. The author of this work has personally seen a baboon in Africa pick up a stick and chase a small boy with it (after the boy had hit the baboon with the same stick). Animals, however, do not know how to make tools for long-term use. This, anthropologists tell us, is a key difference between humans and animals. Humans purposely make tools for long-term and multiple uses.

- Quick Write: As fast as you can, make a list of thirty tools you use every day to make your life easier (for example, car, shoelaces, light switch, etc.). Share your list with the class.
- What If?: For a moment, stop and think of what it would be like to be an early human with absolutely no tools to use. In a short paragraph, describe what it would feel like to be such an early human without any tools. In conclusion, describe the first tool you would make as an early human.
- Pair Share: Divide the class into pair shares (two students working together). Within three minutes, have each pair share make two lists, one of as many simple *wood* tools that early humans could make and one of simple *stone* tools early humans could make. The pair share with the most number of tools at the end of three minutes wins. The accuracy of the winning pair should be checked by having the winning pair share read their list to the class.
- Plenary Session: Conclude by having the class as a whole make a stone and a wooden tool list on the board by adding the suggestions from every group.
- Design Team: Teams of four students should design an "ultimate" stone or wooden tool. Each team's design should be put on a poster board and presented to the class. The best tool designs can be placed on display on the classroom wall.
- ADV Museum Research: Contact local museums to find out if any have displays of early stone and wooden tools used by early humans in your area. If so, plan and conduct a field trip to see these tools.
- ADV Action Research: Check to see if anyone in your community knows how to make stone tools and see if he or she will demonstrate this process to the class.

1.5.2   A Neolithic Ad Campaign

The year is 9000 B.C.E. The location is the Middle East along the Tigris River. Your family is one of the first in the world to start planting wheat and other grain to harvest and eat. Everybody is calling you *Neolithic (New Stone Age)* and laughing at you because your stone tools are not big and bulky, but are rather stone weights with center holes for digging sticks to plant the seeds, and small and sharp stones to cut the wheat in the fall. The trouble is, you need more people to help your family farm the lands, and the local nomads would rather just wander around the hills hunting and looking for wild berries and fruit. They are not very interested in working in the hot fields all day. You need an advertising agency to recruit some of the nomads to come and work in the fields with you.

- Quick Write: Close your eyes for a moment and imagine yourself as an early Neolithic human (9000 B.C.E.) and one of the first human farmers on the planet. In a short paragraph, describe what it feels like to be one of the first farmers in the world.
- Madison Avenue: With a team of four advertising executives (students) from Madison Avenue, develop and present an advertising campaign promoting agriculture (the planting and harvesting of crops) to the hunting and gathering people who live near you (in your class).
- Poster Power: With your ad team, create a large poster promoting the advantages of agriculture over nomadic hunting and gathering.
- Bumper Sticker: Create a bumper sticker that criticizes nomadic hunters and promotes the good life on the farm.
- Counter Sticker: Create a counter sticker that opposes new inventions (such as farming) and wants to return to the good old days when everybody was nomadic.
- ADV Historical Research: Using your school library and the Internet, research one "Neolithic" (key search word) site currently being excavated by archaeologists and report about their findings to the class.

1.6.0   RELIGIOUS THOUGHT

1.6.1   A Poem of Nature

Stand quietly some evening away from the city lights and look at the stars and the crescent moon on the horizon. Sit alone on the beach and listen to the roar of the ocean's waves pounding on the shore. Lie down in a forest some day by yourself and look up at the wind bending the branches and the clouds moving across the sky. Even in our day of jet travel, traffic jams, gigabyte hard drives, and exploring the planet Mars, we can still stand in wonder at the power of nature. From the largest telescope probing our endless universe to the smallest photon in an electron microscope, that wonder at the power of nature still remains. We humans are so small when we try to understand this beautiful chaotic symmetry around us. It is this attempt to understand such a magnificently complex, ever-changing, and yet symmetrical universe that led to the first religious thoughts of early humans. This is a key distinguishing feature that separates human beings from animals—an initial sense of wonder that becomes a scientific curiosity of how things work, and then a religious question of whether a supreme being might be out there someplace guiding everything.

- Quick Write: Think for a moment about nature. In a short paragraph, describe three things that absolutely amaze you about nature.
- Pair Share: When finished with your thoughts about nature, share your thoughts with a partner in the classroom.
- Poet's Corner: As an early human being looking at the universe, write a short poem describing your wonder at what you see.
- Art Mart: As an early human being, create a cave painting on a large piece of paper about the wonders of life you see around you.
- Song Fest: Create a song or a rap that describes your wonder at the universe around you.
- ADV Historical Research: Use your library and the Internet to research what anthropologists think are the earliest forms of religion and share your findings with the class.

1.6.2 Mother Earth

From archaeological evidence and our own language, we have evidence of early human religious beliefs. This evidence focuses on the concept of Mother Earth (Gaia) who controls the human cycle of birth and death, the cycles of the moon, and the yearly cycle of the seasons dying in the fall and rising again in the spring with new life. She went by several different names: Dictynna in ancient Minos on Crete, Artemis in ancient Greece, Diana in classical Rome.

Note from the Future: Most scientists today follow the practice of studying many small parts to try to understand the whole, but some scientists are reversing this and finding evidence that the idea of Mother Earth as a living whole might indeed be true. They call this theory the *Gaia hypothesis* (Capra 1996, 22–23).

- Quick Write: Think for a moment about the name "Mother Earth" and then write a short paragraph describing what you have heard about the "Mother" of nature.
- Pair Share: Share with a partner in class what you have heard about "Mother Earth." Be sure to allow each partner in the pair to talk for at least one minute.
- Concept Web: When the pair share is finished, each pair should share what they said with the class. Two students can act as recorders on the board to develop a class concept web of what we understand about "Mother Nature."
- Front Page: As a team of four student reporters for the *Stone Age Daily News* (an oral campfire news-reporting service), ask several early humans around the campfire (the classroom) what amazes them the most about the wonders of "Mother Earth," and then report your findings in a front-page edition of the newspaper at the next evening campfire.
- Poster Power: Create a poster of your view of how "Mother Earth" might look and of all of the powers she possessed.
- Action Research: Interview parents, neighbors, and friends to gather what impression they have of the "Mother Nature" myth.
- ADV Way Back in Time: The idea of "Mother Earth" dates well before most modern religions. Compare the ancient concept of "Mother Earth" with modern religions. How are they similar and how are they different?
- ADV Gender Bender: Why are the earliest religions we know female oriented and the newer religions male oriented?
- ADV Futurist: Read current research on the Gaia hypothesis, which sees the Earth as a living entity and report back to the class on your findings.

1.6.3   Stonehenge

As early as 10,000 B.C.E., early humans began to formalize their religions by conducting religious services around major stones or forests, and began to erect stone monuments as centers of worship. A magnificent example of such a center is Stonehenge (circa 3000 B.C.E.) in southern England. A prehistoric observatory, the stone monument lines up perfectly with the rising and setting sun at each yearly summer solstice (June 21st, the longest day of the year), when the sun reaches its highest latitude in the sky. From Stonehenge, we can understand that prehistoric humans were quite sophisticated in their knowledge of the universe. They carefully plotted the yearly cycle of the seasons and the points at which the sun set and rose every morning. The builders of Stonehenge must have wondered in awe at the magnificent cycle of life and death in nature that they saw around them, and they based a major part of their religion on what they saw.

• Quick Write: Think of a time when you stood in a quiet spot and watched the sun slowly go down to the horizon. In a short paragraph, describe your feelings as you watched the sun slowly sink and then disappear. What do you think prehistoric humans thought when they witnessed the same daily event of nature?
• Poster Power: Using the illustration or another one you find, create a poster that illustrates what ancient humans must have thought when they witnessed a sunrise at Stonehenge on the summer solstice.
• Model It: Create a diorama or model of a prehistoric monument, such as Stonehenge, out of paper, cardboard, clay, or stone and then label the different parts of your model. If you wish, you can use a flashlight to simulate the sun at summer solstice to illustrate how the real Stonehenge lines up with the rising sun on June 21st each year.
• ADV Prehistoric Research: Research your library and the Internet for "Stonehenge" (key search word) to find out what else you can learn about this magnificent old religious observatory. Be sure to report your findings to your class.

1.7.0   CONQUEST AND WARFARE

1.7.1   Are Humans Violent or Peaceful?

Anthropologists debate whether humans are basically violent or peaceful. As far back as the human record exists, it is clear that humans were often violent toward each other. As recent as the daily news from yesterday, it is clear that humans have a strong tendency toward violence. The question remains, however, whether this violence is natural to human beings toward each other, or whether it is learned and passed from one family to the next. It is also clear from the archaeological record that humans can be peaceful, living in small villages and extended families together, and sharing all work and the food they produce. Humans also enjoy peaceful things, such as art, music, and storytelling. The question whether humans are basically violent or not still remains to be answered (Dubos 1974; Sussman 1997).

- Quick Write: In a short paragraph, describe whether you think humans are basically violent toward one another or basically peaceful toward each other.
- Pair Share: With a partner in class, share (for one minute each) your ideas on whether humans are basically violent or peaceful.
- Bumper Sticker: Are humans basically violent or peaceful? Pick a side, and then create a bumper sticker that supports your position.
- Poster Power: Create a poster that illustrates this disagreement over the basic nature of humans.
- Quick Skit: With a team of four student actors, create a short dramatization of a struggle between two families of early humans over a water hole. Present your dramatization at your next campfire (your next classroom plenary session).
- You Were There: As the ace reporter for the *Stone Age Daily News*, give a play-by-play description of a fight between two early human families over the only water hole within ten miles.
- Stone Age Mediator: Many wars are fought over simple things, such as food and water. Make a list of alternatives the two families might have to fighting over a water hole, and then propose a mediated settlement.
- ADV Historical Research: Using your library and the Internet, research a minimum of two wars and try to identify the root cause of the war. Could it have been avoided? When finished, present your findings to the class at their next campfire.
- ADV The Futurist: Conduct surveys in your school, neighborhood, and on the Internet to inquire as to the possibilities or impossibilities of a future world living without warfare.

1.8.0   TRAGEDY AND DISASTER

1.8.1   Human Survival during the Ice Age

We can only imagine the great tragedies of early humans because we have no written record of these events. The last Ice Age (35,000 to 12,500 B.C.E.) was certainly one of these tragedies. How advanced were human beings before the last Ice Age covered the planet? How many humans, plants, and animal species died because they could not survive the radical drop in the temperature of the planet we call Earth? How many human innovations and ideas were lost because of the vast sheets of ice that covered much of the earth? We actually know very little about how humans survived during the last Ice Age. As the temperature of the Earth plunged, vast amounts of the planet's water became frozen in massive glaciers, and the average sea level dropped as much as ninety feet around the world. Because many Ice Age people lived along the oceans, many of the archaeological human living sites from the Ice Age are currently under water, making them very difficult for archaeologists to excavate.

- Quick Write: Describe in a short paragraph the coldest you have ever been. What did you do to become warm again?
- Bumper Sticker: Create a bumper sticker to hang on trees around the campfire to encourage early humans to think of better ways to keep warm and improve their lives. (In reality, early humans could not read or write, nor did they have pen and paper.)
- Epic Teller of Tales: Oral stories told around the campfire on cold nights were the great literary works of the Ice Age. Imagine yourself as a great Ice Age Epic Teller of Tales and create a grand oral epic of how humans survived during the last Ice Age. You may accompany the epic with a musical instrument or with appropriate music from a CD player.
- The Futurist: As a team of four famed underwater archaeologists from the future, present to your class a report on a major human Ice Age site you have just excavated. Be sure to describe the hazards of excavating underwater, a map of your imaginary excavations, and illustrations of some of your major finds.
- ADV Prehistorical Research: Using your library and the Internet, research what archaeological evidence has been found of human life during the last Ice Age and report back to the class on your findings.

1.8.2   Early Human Cannibalism

Starvation was a constant threat for early humans. Food was scarce—especially in the winter. From archaeological evidence, we know that cannibalism was widely practiced by early humans—due to near starvation. Early humans would even crack open the bones of their dead to suck out the marrow.

- Quick Write: The word *cannibalism* is a frightening word in the English language—or any language. In a short paragraph, describe your feelings and any questions you have when you hear this word.
- Letter to a Friend: As an early human being, write a letter to a friend describing the horror of seeing someone you know being eaten due to starvation.
- Pros and Cons: Do you think cannibalism is justified in times of extreme starvation? Take a position on this question and be prepared to defend it when your class meets again around the campfire.
- Decision Tree: In teams of four students in the class, discuss starvation and cannibalism among early humans in terms of a decision tree to decide what alternative early humans had. The problem "cannibalism" is the trunk of the tree. Each student team thinks of a minimum of three alternatives (branches) early humans had considering starvation and cannibalism. Each team then considers the positive and negative aspects of each alternative (branch). Based on their decision-tree analysis, the team then makes a decision as to the best alternative when faced with starvation and cannibalism.
- ADV Historical Research: Using your library and the Internet, look for modern instances where people have resorted to cannibalism. When finished, report your findings to the class.

1.9.0   EXPLORATION AND DISCOVERY

1.9.1   Fire!

Two major concerns of early humans were getting enough to eat and keeping warm at night, and these two concerns were closely related to each other. The human body gets its energy from eating food and over 90 percent of the body's energy is used in keeping the body warm. If early humans could get more food and keep warmer, they would live a much better life.

Crucial to this equation between food and warmth was the discovery of fire. A few early humans learned about the existence of the phenomena of fire from lightning starting a grass fire. It must have been a frightening experience as the searing heat, smoke, and flames roared through the grass, forcing the animals and early humans to flee for their lives. Early humans also found, however, that this terrible thing called "fire" also had its advantages. Returning a few days later, early humans—always hungry—found that roasted animals trapped and killed by the fire were much easier to eat and tasted rather good. They also found that sleeping by the still-burning embers of an old tree kept them warm at night. Wow, something so dangerous was also so very useful! We can imagine the arguments of early humans: "Stay away from it, it's dangerous!" (conservative position); "No, I like cooked meat and keeping warm at night—let's find out how to use it" (progressive position).

Just imagine what it must have been like to have been an early human to wait around for lightning to start a grass fire before you could have your next cooked meal or heater to keep you warm at night. Some bright young innovator about one million years B.C.E. had a brilliant idea: what if humans keep adding dry wood to a fire to keep it going and take pieces of this fire and build fires elsewhere? Life suddenly became much better due to this major discovery. Early humans with fire as a tool now had more food to eat, because cooked meat was much easier to digest than raw meat. With more food to eat and a nice fire at night to keep them warm, suddenly life was much better for early humans.

- Quick Write: In a short paragraph, describe what it is like to try to eat a piece of raw chicken. From your own experience, tell why you think that cooked chicken is better than raw chicken.
- Poster Power: Create a poster that illustrates both the dangers and the advantages of fire for early humans.
- Madison Avenue: With a team of four student advertisers, develop a worldwide ad campaign to sell early humans on the idea of using fire to cook their meat and keep themselves warm at night.
- Quick Skit: With a team of four student actors, create a short skit that illustrates how early humans lived before and after the discovery of fire.
- ADV Action Research: From the library and the Internet, find out how early humans made fire with a bow, a stick, and dried leaves. Make a fire bow and demonstrate it to your class (outside the classroom). With your demonstration, make a chart that carefully illustrates how to make a fire with a fire bow.

1.9.2   Metal Maker

The early history of humankind is very slow. New human discoveries did not happen very fast. Fire was certainly a major discovery, but that happened about one million years B.C.E. The tools early humans made tell us this very slow story. For several million years, the only tools humans and prehumans made were out of stone and wood. A real change in toolmaking came when someone at the end of the last Ice Age in Serbia, circa 12,500 B.C.E., was trying to make a stone tool, but found that the stone bent instead of chipping or shattering, as had other stones. The toolmaker must have been mad at first, but then began to be curious about this strange stone he could bend by hitting it. The toolmaker suddenly realized that this strange stone lasted longer and could be sharpened easier than stone tools. Something else strange about this bending rock: the toolmaker accidentally dropped it in a fire and it became soft and even easier to bend. This early toolmaker had discovered copper and began the age of metal making.

The problem with copper and tin, however, is that they are very soft and keep bending all sorts of directions when hit too hard. Copper and tin occur together naturally in only two areas of the world: Turkey in the Middle East and Thailand in Southeast Asia. In both Turkey and Thailand, about 4500 B.C.E., an accidental discovery led to a major human advance in toolmaking. In both cases, someone accidentally dropped copper and tin in the same fire at the same time. Imagine their surprise when the two soft metals—copper and tin—melted together and formed a much harder metal called *bronze*. Suddenly, humans had a very strong metal that would not break when dropped, as stone tools did, and would not bend when hit, as copper and tin had. After a million or more years, the Stone Age was now over. Humans had a new source for their tools and weapons—spearheads, plows, knives, kettles, and hundreds of other items could now be made out of bronze. This was the beginning of the Metal Age, with many other metals (such as iron and steel) to be discovered a few thousand years later.

- Quick Write: Think of a moment in your life when you made a major discovery that really surprised you. Write a short paragraph describing your discovery and why it surprised you.
- T Chart: On the left side of your T chart, make a list of tools that could be made with either stone or wood. On the right side of the chart, make a list of tools that could be made with metal.

- Time Traveler: Traveling back in time to the very end of the Stone Age and the beginning of the Metal Age, describe in your diary the momentous change in human history that you are witnessing.
- Song Fest: Make up a song, a rap, or a poem (for nonsingers) about this great discovery of metal making.
- Art Mart: Create a drawing or painting for your classroom wall that illustrates the amazing discovery of bronze.
- ADV Historical Comparison: Using your library and the Internet as sources, compare the discovery of metal making to the other great discoveries of human history, such as agriculture, fire, and human flight. From your research, how does the discovery of metals compare to the other great discoveries of human history and prehistory?

1.10.0   INVENTION AND REVOLUTION

1.10.1   Pottery

The simple invention of pottery in the Middle East (circa 9000 B.C.E.) had an immense impact on humans. For the first time in history, humans could carry water with them when they traveled any distance. For the first time, humans could cook food by soaking it and boiling it in water.

- Quick Write: Make a list of foods that could *not* be prepared and cooked unless you had a pot, bowl, or pan.
- Concept Web: Develop a concept web with the word pottery and list all of the things that early humans and humans today can do with pottery—include nose cones of space shuttles.
- T Chart: Make a T chart focused on the concept of water. On one side of the chart, list items early humans could do with water before they had pottery. On the other side, list all of the things early humans could do with water once they had invented pottery. For example: Without pottery, early humans had to live near water (they could not carry it). With pottery, humans could live in villages safely on hills because water could be carried there in pots.
- Collage: Make a collage of photographs of a minimum of twenty different shapes and uses of pottery: pots, jars, pans, bowls, plates, and sculpture, for example.
- ADV Action Research: Watch someone make a pot on a potter's wheel and then make a simple coiled pot out of clay. As you are making the

pot, imagine that you are the first person in history to make a clay pot. In your diary, then write a short entry describing what it must have felt like to be the first person making a pot.

1.11.0   ART AND CREATIVE THOUGHT

1.11.1   Cave Painting

One of the true indications that humans are different from animals is art. Animals do not make art; humans make art. There is a stereotype that ancient humans lived like primitive animals, concerned only with food, shelter, and an occasional battle with a neighbor. Prehistoric cave and rock paintings from around the world tell us a different story. Many of these rock and cave paintings are some of the true wonders of the world. They often depict a very trained and sophisticated talent at observing nature and a skill at producing something very beautiful.

- Quick Write: Think for a moment about the most beautiful painting you have ever seen. In a short paragraph, describe this painting and share your description with your class.
- Prehistoric Art Mart: On large pieces of paper, have the early humans in your cave (class) become cave painters. Each student should create a simple drawing of a person, animal, or thing.
- Prehistoric Story Line: When each student is finished with the simple drawing, all of the class should stand up in a long line around the room, holding their drawing in front of them. The first student should create a story about the character or animal in their drawing. The imaginary story should then be carried on by the next student—adding onto the story—until every student has had a chance to add to the story.
- Prehistoric Art Gallery: Prehistoric artists with the best drawings can display their work on the cave (classroom) wall; visiting students from other classes may be given a gallery walk of artwork in the class once they are finished.
- ADV Prehistoric Art Walk: Go to the library and find a book on the magnificent cave paintings from Lascaux, France (circa 10,000 B.C.E.). Just wander through the book to look at these magnificent prehistoric works of art. Imagine that you have just discovered the Lascaux caves and keep a log of your impressions of what you see, and share it with the other early humans in your cave (class).

• ADV Prehistoric Art Research: Find other books or Web sites on pre-historic cave and rock paintings from other areas of the world, such as the Tassili Highlands in southern Algeria, Altamira in northern Spain, and the Tsodillo Hills in northwest Botswana. Make a list of the major subjects in each of the paintings at these sites. What similarities and differences are there between these prehistoric paintings from across the world? What kind of materials did each artist mix in their paints? Which do you think are the most beautiful? When finished, describe what you have learned about early prehistoric artwork to the other members of your class.

1.12.0 SUCCESSES AND FAILURES OF THE PREHISTORIC ERA

1.12.1 Race to Prehistoric Success

Quad Race: OK, quads (groups of four students), this is your chance to show your abilities to identify the most important successes of humanity during the prehistoric era.

1. Pick the name of one of the following inventions or discoveries out of a hat for your quad.
2. Then make a long list of reasons why this invention or discovery is the most important during the prehistoric era.
3. When each quad is finished, the teacher will read each quad's list to the class.
4. Each quad should listen carefully to each other quad's answer to ensure that it is acceptable.
5. A scorekeeper will keep count of each quad's point total of acceptable answers on the board.
6. The quad with the most number of acceptable reasons wins the game.
7. The prehistoric inventions and discoveries are as follows:
   • fire
   • stone tools
   • pottery
   • metals
   • towns
8. On your marks, get set, go! (And may the best quad win.)

1.12.2   A Failure to Communicate

Humans created new inventions throughout the prehistoric era. The greatest failure of the prehistoric era was the failure to communicate these new inventions and ideas to others. New discoveries were certainly made, but they were not passed on to others and so died with the inventor.

- Quick Write: How often have you forgotten to tell someone something very important? In a short paragraph, describe such an instance and then share it with the class.
- Poster Power: Develop a poster to place on a tree near the prehistoric campfire (classroom) to encourage early humans to develop better ways of communication.
- Bumper Sticker: Create a bumper sticker encouraging early human beings to share their new ideas with each other.
- Quick Skit: With a team of four early humans (students), create a quick skit that illustrates the need for humans to communicate with each other.
- ADV Historical Research: Look through your library and the Internet for other historical examples of major errors that took place because people failed to let everybody know what they needed to do.

1.13.0   MAJOR WORLD PROBLEMS FOR THE PREHISTORIC ERA

1.13.1   The Utter Poverty of Early Human Beings

The major continuing historical problem of the prehistoric era was the utter poverty of early humans. Every bone discovered by archaeologists from prehistoric humans shows signs of malnutrition. A large number—if not most—of early humans died from starvation during this era. The widespread practice of cannibalism (see TLP 1.8.2) was also an indication of the utter poverty of early humans.

- Quick Write: When you see a homeless person who is unable to take care of him or herself, what reaction do you have? In a short paragraph, describe how you feel about such a person, what you can do to help them, and what they can do to help themselves.
- Poster Power: Create a poster for early humans giving them ideas on new ways to do things so they can escape the terrible poverty of their existence in prehistoric times.

- Front Page: With a team of four student reporters for the *Stone Age Daily Times*, interview early humans (fellow students) from around the campfire (the classroom) to hear different views on how the utter poverty of early human beings can be reduced in the future. When finished, create a front-page edition of your newspaper focusing on this major problem for early humans.
- ADV Action Research: Conduct a campfire (class) project of asking parents, friends, and neighbors about ways early humans could escape the constant starvation they all faced. When completed, discuss the findings of all the students around the campfire. What are the implications of these findings for history and for our own day?

1.14.0   PREHISTORIC ERA ANTECEDENTS FOR THE FUTURE

1.14.1   Is Humankind Ready to Advance?

It is now time to judge whether or not humankind is ready to advance into the next era.

- Viewpoints: Five members from around our campfire will state their basic viewpoints of whether or not enough advancement has been made during the prehistoric era. Should humankind move forward? The five illustrious members are as follows:
  1. Lodak Betrink, the archconservative of the campfire, believes that humankind has gone far enough with enough progress. Betrink believes strongly that the good old days were the best and that humankind needs to hold strongly to past values and beliefs.
  2. Movar Derudzuk, one of the rising young voices at the campfire, is a more moderate conservative who believes that we need to be very cautious with any change and be very sure that no harm will come to the campfire if change takes place. Movar is willing to accept some change, but only in very small amounts and only when the time is right—and wants to decide when that time will come.
  3. Pokaldar Wookbot, the wishy-washy middle-of-the-roader around the campfire, is willing to accept change for a few minutes after one speaker, but might have a change of mind in an instant to oppose change after another speaker has finished.
  4. Yeemul Vatsmeer, the moderate progressive of the group, is willing to support change for the good of the people around the campfire. Vatsmeer is especially in favor of change when Vatsmeer's own family will directly benefit.

5. Quikdok Varull, the radical progressive around the campfire of early humans, is very willing to support any change that will move humanity away from the drafty old prehistoric campfire into something more modern and comfortable for humanity.

- Pick a Position: Each member of early humans (students) around the campfire (classroom) now must chose one of the five positions for humanity to take and support that position with evidence of what they have learned about prehistoric human beings.

- Vote for Humanity: A vote will then be taken of all early humans around the campfire to determine whether or not humanity should move on to the next era. The consensus decision of the imaginary early humans around the imaginary campfire will determine their own future and the rest of humanity. (In reality, just such decisions by early human families were key in deciding whether humans stayed the way they were or progressed to new levels of development.)

Ancient History (4000 B.C.E. to 500 C.E.)

UNIT 2: TABLE OF CONTENTS

INTRODUCTION

The Ancient Era

Humans around 4000 B.C.E. suddenly got their acts together. They discovered and invented more things—such as iron and steel tools—and they told more people about these inventions. Small city-states grew into large empires, and small, local religious beliefs transformed into major religions, such as Hinduism, Judaism, and Christianity. The activities in this chapter share the excitement of the era and have students sense the impact of major inventions, such as writing and the wheel. They will also analyze the significance of some of the major people of these ancient times, the reasons behind the rise and fall of some of the classical civilizations of the world, and the development of the major religions of the world. Through the activities in this chapter, students will discover that the world changed dramatically from prehistoric times, when things had remained the same for centuries. Human beings suddenly improved their existence with new ideas and inventions— such as reading and writing—along with the ability to pass these new ideas and inventions on to others in the future. But students will also learn that change is always not in a positive direction. Large and powerful empires—the Roman Empire, for example—reached their peaks and then eventually fell. Many great ideas, inventions, and writings from Greece and elsewhere in the ancient world were lost through carelessness, war, and just plain apathy.

This is an important chapter of activities because it enables students to realize what humans can do with new ideas, the need to fully communicate these ideas, and the knowledge that even good ideas and empires can fail if not constantly challenged to improve.

THEMATIC LESSON PACS

2.1.0   HISTORICAL TIME LINE

2.1.1   Ancient History Time Line

- Name Plates: Photocopy six sets of the thirteen names and items below. Cut each name or item onto a strip of paper. Place the strips of paper carefully into separate envelopes for each team and label the envelopes "2.1.1 Ancient History Time Line," for later use in class.
- Team Power: Break the class into six teams.
- The Envelope: Each team should be given an envelope containing the following random thirteen names from the ancient era:
  1. Siddhartha Gautama started Buddhism (circa 560 B.C.E.)
  2. Fall of Rome (410 C.E.)

3. Shih Huang Ti built the Great Wall of China (221 B.C.E.)
4. Julius Caesar shifted Rome to an Empire (44 B.C.E.)
5. Hammurabi law code written (circa 2200 B.C.E.)
6. Hindu Upanishads written (circa 400 B.C.E.)
7. Moses established formal Judaism (circa 1300 B.C.E.)
8. Lao Tse started Taoism (circa 604–531 B.C.E.)
9. Invention of writing and wheels (circa 4000 B.C.E.)
10. Jesus started Christianity (circa 30 C.E.)
11. Confucius started social reforms (circa 551–479 B.C.E.)
12. Step Pyramid at Saqqara, Egypt, built (circa 2686 B.C.E.)
13. Pericles established democracy (circa 460–429 B.C.E.)

- Team Time Line: The first job of each team is to correctly order the thirteen names and artifacts according to time, with the oldest at the top and the most recent at the bottom. Each student should separately write the correct time line for the thirteen names and artifacts on a personal sheet of paper for later reference.
- Team Look Up: Once every member of the team has his or her own ancient time line on a sheet of paper, each of the thirteen names should be divided between members of the team to find out the meaning of each name from their textbook. Once found, the meanings of each ancient name or artifact can be shared with the members of their team to write on their own time lines.
- Poster Power: On a large piece of paper, each team should construct its own time line using the thirteen names, with descriptions and illustrations to demonstrate the meaning of each name. When finished, these can be presented to the class and displayed on the classroom wall.
- Music Mart: Each team should pick what they think is the most important name or event in the time line and then compose and present to the team a short song or rap about the name or event. When finished, this can be presented to the class.
- Journal Entry: Have team members write a short journal entry speculating about what they now know about the development of humans during the period from 4000 B.C.E. to 500 C.E.—from the time line they developed—and possibly the most important things to happen during this era. When finished, students can first share their thoughts with their team and then with the class as a whole for a general discussion about what they think are the most important things that happened during the era.

2.2.0   SEPARATING FACT FROM MYTH AND PROPAGANDA

2.2.1   Myth Maker

- Quick Write: Instruct the class to think for a moment of a favorite mythological character and then write a short paragraph about this character.
- Poster Power: Make a poster illustrating the five major archetypes found in human mythology (Pearson 1989). Note that the characters in many comic books and cartoons on TV are archetypes. These five archetypes are as follows:
  1. The Warrior who can conquer any foe
  2. The Martyr who sacrifices his life for a cause
  3. The Magician who has the power to defy nature
  4. The Wanderer who single handedly discovers new worlds
  5. The Villain whose evil deeds darken any day
- Quick Skit: With a team of four student actors, create a short skit that illustrates one of the five major archetypes of mythology.
- ADV Mythological Analysis: Pick one historical person from ancient history, such as Alexander the Great, Attila the Hun, Moses, Jesus, or Cleopatra. Conduct a mythological analysis on that person by reading about that person, and determining whether or not he or she fits one of the five mythological archetypes above. If so, decide whether the person is now more of a myth or still a real historical figure, according to the evidence gathered.

2.3.0   LOCATION AND MOVEMENT

2.3.1   Who, What, and Where Did It First Happen?

Where did the major ancient era inventors and their new ideas come from?

- Pair Share: Divide the class into student pairs (pair shares). Have each pair share pick one person, idea, or invention from the history time line (see 2.1.1) and then speculate on the origins of the idea or invention or on what caused the person to do what he did.
- Look Up: Each pair share should then use their textbook or other source book to locate where the person, idea, or invention started in the world.

- Map Attack: On a blank map of the world, each pair share should indicate this starting point on their map with an illustration of the person, idea, or invention. Each pair share should then share their findings with the rest of the class.
- ADV Historical Research: Using the school library or the Internet, find out how the news of this person, idea, or invention spread around the world and then report your findings to the class.

2.3.2   Great Ideas and Inventions That Did Not Make It

Many of the great ideas and inventions in the world never became well known until a much later date. Why did such great ideas and inventions rapidly spread across the world?

- Pair Share: Using a map of the world, each pair share should brainstorm a minimum of five ways why a great idea or invention from ancient history might fail to spread around the world. (Suggested ideas and inventions include: pyramids, the wheel, iron making, and writing—see 2.1.1.) Each pair share should be sure to think of such geographic barriers as mountains, deserts, and oceans and the lack of any reliable long-distance transportation during ancient history in their discussions.
- Plenary Session: Each pair share should then share their five ways with the class and a recorder should list all of the different ways on the board. The teacher can lead a discussion with the class to decide which five ways are the most likely reasons why an idea or invention failed to spread for such a long time.

2.4.0   POLITICS AND LEADERSHIP

2.4.1   Pyramid Power (2600 B.C.E.)

Organized central states can do things that small groups of people in villages cannot do. After 3000 B.C.E., humans were suddenly doing very large organized projects that early humans did not even dream of—such as building pyramids. They were the world's first symbols of the power of a centralized state. The pharaohs were buried in the pyramids as symbols of the state, not for their own glory. The great pyramids of Egypt, contrary to myth, were not built with slave labor but by free Egyptians working three months each year while the Nile was flooded (Boorstin 1992, 88).

- Quick Write: In your mind, imagine standing next to the great pyramids at Giza in Egypt. In a short paragraph, describe what you think about these gigantic stone monuments.
- Pair Share: In student pairs, brainstorm for two minutes and make a list of five things people can do with a pyramid. (This is really a trick question. Pyramids are really not very useful.)
- Strategy Session: Student quads (teams of four students each) should brainstorm and plan strategies on what it would take to have people from all over Egypt work together on a large project (such as a pyramid) three months at a time for ten years.
- Poster Power: Create a large poster encouraging the people of Egypt to cooperate and build one of the great pyramids of Egypt more than 4,000 years ago.
- Bumper Sticker: Create a funny bumper sticker to encourage the Egyptians building the pyramids to enjoy their work.
- Speech Writer: As a bright and upcoming pharaoh-to-be of Egypt, write a speech to your countrymen urging them to keep building pyramids as a means of keeping the country together.
- Political Rally: Stage a pro-pyramid political rally in your classroom—with banners, posters, and speeches—promoting the building of more pyramids.
- The Futurist #1: Times have changed. What do you think it would take to get anybody to volunteer the time to build a pyramid today? Conduct a poll in your school and neighborhood to see how many people would volunteer to help build a pyramid. When completed, report your findings to the class.
- ADV The Futurist #2: During the early fourth dynasty of Egypt, the pyramids were the symbol of the power of the state. Research your library and the Internet to identify the symbols of power of the state today.

2.4.2   Hammurabi's Laws (circa 2200 B.C.E.)

Hammurabi, the first king of Babylon, also wrote the first known law code. Two of Hammurabi's laws were as follows (Harper 2000):

1. #3: "If any one brings an accusation of any crime before the elders, and does not prove what he has charged, he shall, if it be a capital offense, be put to death."
2. #22: "If any one is committing a robbery and is caught, then he shall be put to death."
    - Quick Write: In a short paragraph, describe what you think it might have been like to live in a time that did not have any laws.
    - Quick Skit #1: With a team of four students, write a short skit depicting what it would be like without any written laws and present it to the class.
    - T Chart: Create a T chart that compares things that happen when people do not have laws (for example, stealing somebody's food) and then how this would be different if laws existed.
    - Poster Power: Create a poster that encourages people to create laws and to live and work together peacefully.
    - Quick Skit #2: In a team of four students, create a short skit that illustrates what it might have been like to live under Hammurabi's laws (2200 B.C.E.). When finished, speculate how these laws are different from our laws today.
    - The Futurist: With a partner, rewrite Hammurabi's laws so they could possibly be used today and present them to your class.
    - ADV Historical Research: Using your library and the Internet, research other examples of Hammurabi's laws in early Babylon and share them with the class.

2.4.3   The First Female Pharaoh

Hatshepsut was one of the first great women in our historical record. Foreigners called the *Hyksos* (shepherd kings) had ruled northern Egypt for a hundred years after 1700 B.C.E. As the pharaoh after the death of her husband, Thutmose II, she drove the Hyksos out of Egypt, and reestablished a strong, centralized Egyptian government based in Thebes. She was not only an able ruler, she also had artistic taste and had the most beautiful temple in Egypt constructed across the Nile from Thebes. All, however, were not pleased with her rule. Her stepson, Thutmose III, resented her rule; when she died, he quickly covered up her name with plaster on every monument he could find, and replaced her name with his name. Thanks to the plaster protection with which Thutmose III coated his stepmother's statues, we know a great deal about Hatshepsut due to her many well-preserved monuments (see Canby 1961).

- Quick Write: In a short paragraph, present your opinion of women being strong leaders of countries.
- Bumper Sticker: Create a bumper sticker either for or against one of the great female rulers in history, Hatshepsut.
- Quick Skit: With a team of four students, present a short skit that illustrates the rule of Egypt's first female pharaoh.
- Front Page: With a team of four, develop a front-page edition of the *Classical Times* newspaper that focuses on the rule of the Pharaoh Hatshepsut.
- You Were There: As the host of this popular TV program, have the studio audience each write down one question for them to interview this week's guest, Hatshepsut (a student in costume), visiting us from over 3,500 years ago.
- What If?: What if Hatshepsut visited our country today? What would she say about the role women have in our country's politics? Write a short speech you think she might give on this topic.
- ADV Historical Research: Using the library and the Internet, find other major women rulers who made important contributions to their nation's well-being. When finished, report your findings to the class.

2.4.4 Volcanoes, Hyksos, and Hebrews?

There is no historical record of a Hebrew people in Egypt except for the Bible. Many historians, however, believe that the biblical Hebrews were one of the shepherd tribes of the Hyksos, who were the foreign rulers of northern Egypt for one hundred years at the end of the Middle Kingdom (circa 1700–1600 B.C.E.). A major, early Hyksos archaeological site exists in southern Israel. Circumstantial evidence from the Greek island of Thera (Santorini) also ties the Hebrews to the Hyksos. Egyptian artifacts from the era of Pharaohs Hatshepsut and Thutmose III (circa 1630 B.C.E.) date from the remains found on Thera at the time of the gigantic volcanic explosion (1628 B.C.E.)—one of the largest in history—that destroyed most of the island. If matched to the biblical stories in Exodus—dark skies, a pillar of fire, and a tidal wave—the volcanic eruption 400 miles to the north might provide some confirmation to the stories of Moses. Exodus says that Moses parted the waters of the Red Sea. Could this have been a tidal wave? Although the Red Sea is not part of the Mediterranean, the written word "Reed" is very close to "Red" in Hebrew. A "Sea of Reeds" is a major location in northern Egypt along the Mediterranean and would have been directly affected by a tidal wave from Thera. A simple copying mistake by a scribe thousands of years ago could explain this possible change of location.

Also according to Egyptian records, the former Hyksos rulers (Moses and the Hebrews?) were chased out of Egypt by Hatshepsut and her stepson, Thutmose III. The Hebrew version of the story says they were escaping from Egyptian slavery. Exodus also mentions that Moses was raised as a royal prince in Egypt. His name, Moses, has a great deal of similarity to another royal prince of the same time, named Thut-*mose*. Were they related? We do not know, but with other circumstantial evidence tying together the Hebrews with the Hyksos, it might be possible (Pellegrino 1993; Assmann 1997).

- Quick Write: Imagine for a moment a gigantic volcanic explosion near your town. In a short paragraph, describe what reactions you would have in such an instance and what you would do.
- Map Attack: Using an atlas and a blank map of the Mediterranean area, locate the Greek island of Thera (Santorini) just north of Crete. Then, simulating the volcanic eruption on Thera, draw a circle 400 miles in circumference around the island to indicate the area where volcanic ash from the volcano likely fell. How much of Egypt would have been effected by this explosion? Looking at your map, could a tidal wave from the volcano have hit Egypt?
- Bumper Sticker: Create two bumper stickers: one for the Egyptian version of the chasing of the Hyksos rulers (Hebrews?) out of Egypt and the other for the Hebrew version of escaping from Egyptian slavery.
- Quick Skit: With four student actors from the classroom, create a short drama that illustrates the difference in interpretations between the Egyptians and the Hebrews about the Hyksos (if they were indeed Hebrew).
- ADV Interpretive Research: Through classroom discussion and research in the library, try to explain why peoples such as the Egyptians and the Hebrews would have different interpretations of the same events in which both people took part.

2.4.5   Greek Democracy

Our concept of democracy comes from the ancient Greeks in the time of Pericles (circa 460–429 B.C.E.). Let us recreate that period of history. Your classroom is now the classical city-state of Athens and your classmates are the citizens of Athens:

- Quick Write: In a short paragraph, describe what you think is meant by the word "democracy."
- Amphitheater: Rearrange the desks in the class into concentric circles facing the front to represent an ancient Greek amphitheater. Twenty thousand of the leading citizens of Athens have gathered here in our amphitheater to debate the major issues of the day. Listen to the excitement of the crowd. With the person next to you, make a list of topics you think might be discussed by these citizens of Athens.
- Dictatorship or Democracy: Make believe that you are a citizen of ancient Athens. The people of the city have gathered to decide whether they want to live under a dictatorship or under a democracy. You have been asked to be one of the major speakers to speak either in favor of democracy or dictatorship. Pick the form of government you will support. Write a strong, short speech calling for the people of Athens to support your choice and deliver it in front of the gathered citizens of Athens (students in the class).
- The Rowdy Crowd of Athens: The Athenian crowd (students) may cheer, boo, or hiss their favorite (or not so favorite) speakers as they speak.
- Take a Vote: When all the speeches are finished, the citizens of Athens may then vote on whether they want to live under a dictatorship or a democracy.
- ADV Historical Research #1: Analyze the following quote. Shah Cyrus of Persia commented on the political organization of the Greeks after he had conquered them: "I have never yet been afraid of any men, who have set a place in the middle of their city, where they could come together to cheat each other and tell one another lies under oath" (Boorstin 1992, 96). What did he mean?
- ADV Historical Research #2: Using your library and the Internet, compare dictatorships and democracies as political systems. What are the advantages and disadvantages of each? When finished, describe which one you think is a superior political system and share your thoughts with your class.

2.4.6   The Great Wall of China

Great walls have been used throughout history in an attempt to keep people from crossing borders into other countries. Shih Huang Ti, the first emperor of China during the Ch'in Dynasty (221 B.C.E.) constructed the first Great Wall we know of in order to keep the Mongols out of China. It is the longest and most massive human structure in the world and the only one that can be seen from space. Other large historical walls include the following:

1. Hadrian's Roman Wall (circa 122 C.E.) to keep the Scots out of England
2. The Maginot Line (1914) to keep the German troops out of France before World War I
3. The Berlin Wall (1949–1989) to keep East Germans from fleeing to West Berlin, Germany
4. The Tijuana Wall (1996 to the present) to stop Mexican illegal immigrants from entering the United States
   - Quick Write: In a short paragraph, describe what you would think of a neighbor of yours who put up a tall cement wall between his house and yours. Why do you think the neighbor put up the wall?
   - Map Attack: Using your textbook or a historical atlas and a blank map of Asia, draw the Great Wall of China and measure its length.
   - Poster Power: Create a poster to attach to the Great Wall (of your classroom) that illustrates why the Great Wall of China was first built.
   - Graffiti: On a large piece of butcher paper, create a saying that might have been placed on the Great Wall as graffiti.
   - Wall Simulation: Walls are very intimidating structures and can change the way people interact with each other:
     1. Divide your class in half with a wall of chairs, with only one entryway where students can pass through the wall.
     2. Half of the class (the Groks) will stand on one side. The other half of the class (the Zulls) will stand on the other side.
     3. Each Grok and Zull should keep a journal to record his or her feelings at each stage of this activity. They can record their initial feelings now that a wall separates them.

4. The Groks and the Zulls should each design a badge or paper hat indicating who they are.
5. The Groks and Zulls should write slogans and tape them on the wall describing why their side of the wall is better than the other.
6. The Groks and the Zulls can write and sing a rap or a song about what they think of each other.
7. Groks and Zulls can e-mail messages to any remaining friends they might have on the other side of the wall describing what they feel about the wall.
8. The Groks and the Zulls should each make special rules for when one of the others want to pass through their territory, and any other rules they think necessary to keep their territory free from the other group.
9. Timeout should now be called to have each Grok and Zull write a journal entry about what is happening.
10. After the journal writing has been completed, the wall should be taken down and students take their regular seats.
11. The activity now needs to be debriefed. How were the Groks and the Zulls beginning to feel about each other? What would start to happen if the wall was left up for several days?
12. Each student (Groks and Zulls) should write concluding essays examining what the wall did to the class. Students should also speculate as to what happens when such a wall is constructed in history.
   • ADV Historical Research: Use the library and the Internet to find pictures and stories of the walls that were constructed by one country to keep a certain group of people from crossing a border. In your research, find evidence as to whether each wall was successful or not. When finished, report to the class on whether or not this strategy of constructing walls was successful or not.

2.5.0 SOCIAL AND ECONOMIC LIFE

2.5.1 Ancient Civilization Travel Promotion

It must have been fascinating to be alive during one of the great classical civilizations of ancient times.

- In groups of four students each, pick one of the great civilizations of ancient times (such as classical Egypt, Mesopotamia, Greece, or Rome) and develop a promotional travel campaign to that civilization. Be sure to use your textbook, library, and the Internet for information on your civilization. Your promotional campaign should include the following:
  1. A large map of the civilization
  2. A poster advertising travel to that civilization
  3. A presentation of what to go and see in the civilization
  4. An analysis of what was strong and what was weak about the civilization
  5. A list of ideas and inventions we acquired from that civilization
- When you are finished with your travel promotion, your team may present it to the class.

2.6.0   RELIGIOUS THOUGHT (4000 B.C.E. TO 500 C.E.)

The major religions of the world appear during this classical period of history. The following activities focus on understanding the major ideas of each religion or religious leader as they appear chronologically in history—Hinduism, Moses and Judaism, Buddha, Lao Tse, Confucius, and Jesus and Christianity. (The rise of Christianity and Muhammad and Islam will be considered later during the Middle Ages in unit 3.)

2.6.1   Hinduism

There is no one belief or dogma in Hinduism. Everyone can create a new god—this is acceptable in Hinduism. Even Jesus is acceptable in Hinduism as a god. Hindus believe that the splendor of the world is so vast that no one god could have made it all. In such a complex world, the more gods, the better. In this complex of many gods, a trinity of three major gods exists—a supreme, but distant father figure named Brahma, who is above everything; Vishnu, a god of life and vitality; and Shiva, a god of death and rebirth. Life and death, however, are not permanent for a Hindu—they are a cycle of birth and rebirth, of being born into the next life with each life hopefully better than the last one. The idea of worship is also quite different between Hindus and Christians. Hindus do not go to a temple (church) to worship. In Christianity, worshipers enter their church (temple) to hear and read the word of God. Hindus, instead, stand outside the temple and look in to see the image (or dar'san) of god in the temple and present fruit as offerings.

In the beginning (what Christians call "Creation"), Hindus believe that everything was together as one in nature. While Christians have the goal to go to a place called "Heaven," it is the aim of every Hindu eventually to return to a state of oneness with nature.

- Quick Write: Imagine that you are a Hindu. As a Hindu, you must choose the most important things in life to you. Once you have made that decision, you may pick the gods you wish to worship to assist you with these important things—but you may worship only one god at a time. In a short paragraph, describe the most important things in life to you and what things you would like to see in the god or gods you choose.
- Poster Power: Create a poster that illustrates your impression of the Hindu idea of the cycle of death and rebirth, and the eventual hope to go back to being at one with nature.
- T Chart: With a T chart, compare the Hindu form of worship to the Christian concept of worship, based on the information in the previous paragraph.
- Venn Diagram: Use a Venn diagram to compare the differences and similarities of this Hindu idea of creation with that of the Christian concept of creation, using the information in the above paragraph.
- Field Trip: If a Hindu temple exists near your home, take a field trip there and then write a report to the class on what you saw.
- Art Mart: Find a picture and a description of a Hindu god in your library or on the Internet, and draw a picture of this god in a temple so that others can see his *dar'san*.
- ADV Religious Comparison #1: Using sources in your library and on the Internet, compare the three major gods in Hinduism (Brahma, Vishnu, and Shiva) to the three parts of the Christian God (Father, Son, and Holy Ghost). Develop a Venn diagram to illustrate the similarities and differences between them.
- ADV Religious Comparison #2: Develop a poster illustrating your understanding of the differences between Hinduism and Christianity.

2.6.2   Lao Tse (circa 604–531 B.C.E.)

Lao Tse, in his Tao Te Ching, set the direction of Chinese religion for more than 1,200 years. His teachings and philosophy were the ultimate in simplicity.

- Reader's Corner: To set the mood to read from the Tao Te Ching, be sure everyone is quiet. Have soft music playing in the background. Have an excellent reader recite the following passage to the class, softly with feeling (Tsu 1972):

Better stop short than fill to the rim.
Oversharpen the blade, and the edge will soon blunt.
Amass a store of gold and jade, and no one can protect it.
Claim wealth and titles, and disaster will follow.
Retire when the work is done.
This is the way of heaven.

- Contemplation: Be sure the students have a moment of quiet after the passage is read to contemplate what was said. Read each line separately and ask the students to record on paper what the line means to them.
- T Chart: With a T chart, compare the American ideal of successful man or woman with the teaching of Lao Tse.
- Time Traveler: Imagine a Chinese time machine bringing Lao Tse to the United States today. What would he say about life in America?
- Finding Ch'i: Go outside and draw a tree on a piece of paper to see if you can feel the ch'i of the tree and nature. European painters found the beauty of landscape painting (ch'i) during the 1700s (twelve hundred years after Lao Tse).
- ADV Comparing Art: Using sources in your library, look at the great early paintings of Europe's best painters—Michelangelo, Velasquez, and Rubens. They painted great people of importance. Look at the works of the great painters of China; they painted landscapes. Chinese painters sought the simple Taoist ideal of balancing the opposites of life (yin and yang) to obtain oneness with nature (ch'i).
- ADV Religious Comparison: Using a T chart, compare the ideals of Lao Tse and the "Taoist religion" with what you know of Christianity.
- ADV Reader's Corner: Check out a copy of Lao Tse's *Tao Te Ching* from your school library, find a favorite quiet corner, and read it to experience a sense of ch'i (oneness with nature).

2.6.3   The Buddha (Born circa 560 B.C.E.)

Prince Siddhartha Gautama (the Buddha), from India, was born into great wealth, but was shocked when he witnessed the poverty and suffering of most of his fellow human beings. Siddhartha's answer was not to try and improve the world but to escape from suffering through enlightenment (nirvana). This enlightenment or nirvana for the Buddha was to end suffering by not craving earthly things. Asoka, the king of the Mauryan Empire in India, was the first major ruler to convert to Buddhism (321 B.C.E.), after being horrified by the massive deaths caused by warfare. Asoka and Buddhists throughout history have remained nonviolent. The famous short novel Siddhartha (about the Buddha) by Herman Hesse gives a good description of the self-imposed sufferings that humans put on themselves during this life, and the enlightenment or nirvana needed to end this suffering.

> Siddhartha now also realized why he had struggled in vain with his Self. Too much knowledge had hindered him; too many holy verses; too much doing and striving. He had been full of arrogance; he had always been the cleverest, the most eager—always a step ahead of the others, always the learned and intellectual one. Now he understood it and realized that the inward voice had been right, that no teacher could have brought him salvation. That was why he had to go into the world, to lose himself. That is why he had to be a merchant, a dice player, a drinker, and a man of property. That is why he had to undergo those horrible years, suffer nausea, learn the lesson of the madness of an empty, futile life till the end, till he reached bitter despair, so that Siddhartha the pleaser-monger and Siddhartha the man of property could die. He had died and a new Siddhartha had awakened from his sleep. He also would grow old and die, but today he was young, he was a child—the new Siddhartha—and he was very happy. (Hesse 1951)

- Quick Write #1: Make a list of ten favorite people you love and ten favorite things you own.
- Pair Share #1: In a pair share, talk about these favorite people and things with a fellow student and then share them with the class.
- Quick Write #2: In a short paragraph, describe how you would feel if all of these people and things were no longer available to you.
- Pair Share #2: In a pair share, discuss your suffering due to the loss of your favorite people and things. Note: This is the suffering for material things spoken of by the Buddha. The aim of *nirvana* is to do without these feelings of want for earthly things.
- Meeting of the Minds: For a classroom presentation, stage a meeting between a typical TV couch potato/junk-food fanatic of today and the Buddha from 2,500 years ago. Have each member of the class write down a question to ask each guest.

- Time Traveler: As a time traveler, bring the Buddha to your hometown today and have him describe what he sees in your material world through Buddhist eyes.
- Front Page: As the ace reporter for the *Ancient Times* newspaper, write a newspaper article from 321 B.C.E. describing Asoka's conversion to Buddhism and present it to your class.
- ADV Religious Comparison: Using your library and the Internet as resources, research the similarities and differences between Buddhism and Christianity, and make a Venn diagram comparing the two.
- ADV Poet's Corner: Read *Siddhartha* by Herman Hesse for a short, simple story of the life of the Buddha. After finishing this little book, write a poem describing your feelings about life through the eyes of Siddhartha.

2.6.4   Confucius (circa 551–479 B.C.E.)

Many Westerners are confused about Confucius. He did not found a religion. He was not concerned with creation, worship, or the idea of god. He had no commandments or rules to follow. He was never a crusader or a leader in battle. The teaching of Lao Tse had become the major religion in China. The teachings of Confucius, however, were more of a social movement than a religion. His sayings were—and still are—a means of improving how we can serve our fellow humans. The following readings are from his *Great Learning* (Confucius 1971):

> When the mind is not present, we look and do not see; we hear and do not understand; we eat and do not know the tastes of what we eat.
>
> 1. Riches adorn a house, and virtue adorns the person. The mind is expanded, and the body is at ease. Therefore, the superior man must make his thoughts sincere.
> 2 From the loving example of one family, a whole state becomes loving, and from its courtesies the whole state becomes courteous, while from the ambition and perverseness of one man, the whole state may led to rebellious disorder—such is the nature of the influence. This verifies the saying: "Affairs may be ruined by a single sentence; a kingdom may be brought down by one man."

- Quick Write: In a short paragraph, write down and describe the meaning of a favorite saying of yours.

- Bumper Sticker: Create a bumper sticker honoring the wisdom of Confucius.
- Poster Power: Create a poster illustrating the meaning of each of the sayings of Confucius.
- TV Talk Show Host: Imagine you were a famous talk show host and Confucius (a member of your class) has agreed to appear on your show. Have each member of your studio audience be prepared to ask him a question.
- Role Play: Imagine you are Confucius visiting the United States today. What would you say about how people lived? What recommendations would you have for Americans? In a class plenary session, tell the class what you would say to Americans today.

2.6.5 Judaism

In the book of Exodus 2:1–10, we can see the beginnings of monotheism and Judaism in a magical leader from Egypt named Moses (circa 1300 B.C.E.). The God of Moses had no name and he appeared to Moses at the top of a mountain to give the Jewish people the ten rules by which they must live. Several of the rules that God gave Moses on the mountain were as follows:

1. Thou shalt worship no other gods before thee.
2. Thou shalt not kill.
3. Thou shalt make no statues of any living thing for I am a jealous God.

The Jewish God also had no hesitation about going to war. Moses sang to his God (Exodus 15:6–7):

Thy right hand, O Lord, glorious in power.
Thy right hand, O Lord, shatters the enemy.
In the greatness of thy majesty thou overthrowest thy adversaries.
Thou sendest forth thy fury, it consumes them like stubble.

Many of the early religions of the world practiced human sacrifice. The god of the Jewish people, however, was different and outlawed the practice of sacrificing humans (Genesis 22:1–19). Many other people, such as the Greeks and Romans, believed that men could become gods.

This, however, was not so with the Jewish religion. Jewish holy men, such as Moses, could perform magic, miracles, and rise to heaven without dying, but men could not become God, not even Moses, the holiest man of Judaism. Greek and Roman rulers, on the other hand, regularly proclaimed themselves to be gods. For many years, Rome ruled the central part of the Jewish homeland—Judea—and insisted on placing statues of their Roman emperor/gods inside the main Jewish temple in Jerusalem. We can only imagine the anger of the traditional Jewish religious leaders—opposed to having more than one god, opposed to statues, and opposed to men becoming gods—at having statues of a Roman emperor/god in their temple.

Historical Note: It was this same Jewish/Roman struggle that Jesus was involved in during his lifetime.

- Quick Write: In a short paragraph, describe Moses' vision of his monotheistic God.
- Poster Power: Create an illustration of Moses meeting his God on Mount Sinai.
- Map Attack: Using an atlas and a blank map of the Middle East, locate Egypt (the birthplace of Moses), Mount Sinai in the Sinai Peninsula in modern Egypt, and Judea/Israel (the traditional home of the Jewish people).
- Ace Reporter: Imagine yourself as a reporter for the local *Sinai Papyrus* newspaper. With another student, develop a spirited interview between the news-papyrus reporter and Moses after he comes down from the mountain. When finished, present this interview of the millennium to the class.
- Role Play: Imagine that your class is now a courtroom in Roman Judea where a panel of neutral judges (students) has been called in to arbitrate the ongoing battle between the Jewish people and the Roman rulers.
  1. Two teams of lawyers (students)—one team representing the Jewish leaders, the other team representing the Romans—will prepare arguments for arbitration judges in order to settle the fighting between the Jewish radicals and the Romans. (Both the Jewish leaders and the Romans [in our fictional recreation] have agreed to abide by the rulings of the court.)
  2. The lawyers and the judges should focus on the facts that the Jewish leaders believe in only one God, that no man can become God, and that no statue of God can be erected. The lawyers and the

judges, on the other hand, should focus on the fact that the Roman emperor has declared himself to be god and wants his statue to sit in the Jewish temple.

Historical Note: In reality, the Romans finally got tired of Jewish opposition to their rule and leveled Jerusalem, the capital of the Jews, in 69–70 C.E.

- ADV Religious Comparison #1: In a quick write, compare the Jewish concepts of worshiping only one God and of making no statues with the Hindu beliefs of having many gods with statues to see (dar'san) only, and not worship.
- ADV Religious Comparison #2: Compare the teachings of the God of Moses with the teachings of Buddha and Lao Tse with a T chart. Why do you think these religions are so different?
- ADV Religious Comparison #3: Compare the Jewish teachings of a monotheistic God (no human sacrifice, and no humans becoming God) with the Christian teachings of a three-in-one God (the sacrifice of Jesus on the cross, and Jesus being God and man at the same time).

2.6.6   Alexandria (265 B.C.E.–59 C.E.)

Poor Alexandria (Egypt) gets mistakenly overlooked in many world history textbooks. Alexandria was the intellectual capital (not Athens or Rome) of the classical Mediterranean world for more than 300 years. An exciting mixture of Greek, Jewish, and Egyptian thinkers of Alexandria made several major contributions to world history and especially world religion.

1. The lighthouse of Alexandria—one of the first in the world—was one of the wonders of the ancient world.
2. The Great Library of Alexandria—another wonder of the ancient world—had more than 500,000 scrolls containing the major writings of the classical world.

    Historical Note: Only a few hundred of the scientific, poetic, religious, and historical works stored in this great library are still with us today, 2,000 years later.
3. The Jews, even in the ancient world, were known for their old religion. The Greeks were known especially for their philosophy. The Jewish religion and the philosophy of the Greeks met in Alexandria, with some very large repercussions for both the Jewish and

Christian religions. One result of this Jewish/Greek meeting in Alexandria was that over 100 Jewish/Greek scholars translated the Jewish Bible (Old Testament) into Greek during the reign of Ptolemy II (circa 265–246 B.C.E.). It became known as the *Septuagint.* The Greek writers of the Christian New Testament (60–150 C.E.), including Paul, used this Septuagint (not the Hebrew Bible) in their work.

4. A Jew by the name of Philo of Alexandria (circa 25 B.C.E.–50 C.E.) created the concept of "theology" by explaining Judaism through Greek philosophy and the use of "allegory." (Note: Allegory is the explaining of something, not by what appears on the surface words, but through hidden meanings and references.) Philo's use of allegory enabled Christians to use both the Old Testament and Greek philosophy to explain their religion. Simple Biblical stories could now be analyzed allegorically for deeper hidden meanings. Philo also developed the concept of "Logos"—the idea that the "word of God" is God (Boorstin 1992, 52).

- Quick Write: Think of a time in your life when you saw two different ideas merge together to become a powerful new idea. Describe this in a short paragraph, and share it with the class when finished.
- Poet's Corner: Imagine you are an ancient Greek sailor on the Mediterranean Sea late at night, and you see this magical light on the horizon. You know that this is the light from the Great Lighthouse at Alexandria. In free verse poetry, describe what this light during the night means to you.
- Art Mart: Create a drawing or painting of what the Great Library at Alexandria might have looked like when it contained most of the great writings of the classical world.
- Letter Home: Imagine you are the first time traveler to visit the Great Library of Alexandria in 200 B.C.E. In a letter back home to your class, describe what it means to be in the biggest library in the classical world.
- Poet's Corner: In a poetic "Ode to Alexandria," describe what it has meant to the world to have lost forever most of the world's knowledge during the classical times.
- ADV Biblical Scholar: Imagine yourself as a Biblical scholar following the ideas of Philo. Look through the Christian New Testament

and find a minimum of three stories that can be told simply at the surface level and then allegorically at a deeper level to explain a religious principle. (Example: Matthew 13:3–9 "Some [seed] fell on rocky soil." Allegorically, Matthew (through Jesus) explained that, in this parable, "seed" referred to people who refused to believe in God.)

- ADV Religious Comparison: Christians, however, with a complex three-in-one God, needed allegorical explanation in their developed theology. Using sources in your library, trace the development of the concept of "theology" with the rise of Christianity.

    Historical Note: Hindus and Buddhists did not need theology and allegory to explain their religions.

2.6.7   Jesus Himself

Jesus, from the stories in the Bible and from archaeological evidence (Crossan 1991; Silberman 1994), was obviously a poor Jewish rabbi with the radical idea to purify the Jewish faith by taking back the temple in Jerusalem from the corrupt high priests and Roman sympathizers. He taught that "The poor shall inherit the earth." He tried to "purify" the main temple in Jerusalem from Roman influence by force, but failed (Matthew 21:12). As with many others who rebelled against Roman rule during the period, Jesus was promptly executed by crucifixion.

- You Were There: As the top-flight anchorperson for the popular marketplace panel show called "You Were There" in 33 C.E., conduct a show covering the recent crucifixion of a Jewish radical rabbi called *Jesus*. For your panel show, you will need five prominent local participants (from the class):
    1. Simon Cleophus, an assistant to the chief priest
    2. Maximus Vainius, an officer in the Roman army
    3. Drusilla Felixus, an upper-class Greek lady (pro-Roman)
    4. Zaddik the Nazarene, a radical follower of Jesus
    5. Aeneas Nailemhigh, a local cross maker

    Members of the marketplace (the class) should each develop a probing set of questions for each panel member. The panel members may also come in costume.

2.6.8 Jesus, the God

The followers of Jesus claim to have seen Jesus after his death by crucifixion, and that he rose into heaven shortly afterward. Paul (died circa
66 C.E.) and other followers taught that God sent his son, Jesus, down
from heaven to become man and save everybody by sacrificing or mar-
tyring himself on the cross.

About 100 C.E., Christian writers such as John began to develop a
full theology for Christianity following Philo of Alexandria. They used
Philo's concept of "allegory" to see hidden meanings in the Jewish
Bible (Old Testament). They also used Philo's concept of "Logos" or
"the word" as God. Christians applied this concept of Logos to Jesus
and saw that he was the "word of God" (Logos) and therefore God himself (John 1:1–14). The early debate between different groups of Christians on whether Jesus was a human messiah (savior), such as Moses,
or God was a major one and led to early divisions within the Church.
Eventually, Emperor Constantine called for the leaders of Christianity
to come to Nicaea (325 C.E.) and decide this issue. After much debate,
the bishops voted and a majority of mostly Eastern bishops agreed to
the concept of a three-in-one (trinity) God—Father, Son, and Holy
Ghost.

- Poster Power: Create a poster that illustrates the struggle within the
  early church to decide whether Jesus was God, man, or both.
- Venn Diagram: Make a Venn diagram to compare the similarities and
  differences between the major teachings of Judaism (see 2.6.5) and
  Christianity. Be sure to compare the concepts of human sacrifice and
  humans becoming God.
- ADV Five-Way Comparison: Make a chart comparing the major features of the following religions: Hinduism, Buddhism, Taoism, Judaism, and Christianity (see 2.6.1–2.6.8).
- ADV Poster Power: Note the key difference between Hindus who
  wish to see a vision (or *dar'san*) of God and Christians who want to
  hear the word of God because they believe that the word or Jesus *is*
  God. Create a poster illustrating these very fundamental differences
  between Hinduism and Christianity. What are some possible implications of this great difference between religions in the future?
- ADV Essay: Using your chart and poster, write an essay describing
  the major similarities and differences between these classical religions of the world.

(Note: The *rise* of Christianity and Islam will be covered in chapter 4.)

2.7.0 CONQUEST AND WARFARE

2.7.1 The Ancient Greek Warrior

From as early as the great epic tales of Homer, the Greeks took pride in their soldiers and their great battles such as Troy, where Greek soldiers hid themselves inside a wooden Trojan horse and secretly opened the gates of the city for the waiting invaders outside. Most early Greek battles were fought only between the strongest individual soldiers on both sides of a battle. Their helmets, armor, weapons, and shields were made out of heavy bronze and they would often fight until one of the combatants died. Death for such brave warriors was considered to be full of valor and honor for their family, in order to lessen the sorrow and grief of loved ones.

- Quick Write: In a short paragraph, create a description of a mythical warrior who can vanquish any foe and conquer any land.
- Diary Entry: As a Bronze Age warrior from ancient Greece, imagine what it feels like to go into battle dressed as described. If you wish, read your diary entry to the class when finished.
- Bumper Sticker: Create a bumper sticker for ancient-era warriors of Greece to put on their heavy bronze armor.
- Poster Power: Create an advertising poster to recruit more Bronze Age warriors into one of the armies of the Greek city-states.
- Quick Skit: In a team of four student actors, create a short skit that illustrates what it might have been like marching off to war with several hundred other Bronze Age warriors from one of the classical Greek city-states.
- ADV Action Research: Conduct a series of interviews in your class, in your school, and in your neighborhood to see if people view "war" as something to be glorified or something to be resisted at all possible costs.

2.7.2 Alexander the Great

At the age of twenty-two, the amazing Alexander the Great (356–323 B.C.E.) of Macedonia led his army on a ten-year march in which he traveled over 2,800 miles and conquered most of the Middle East. He never had more than 100,000 people under his command, and yet was able to conquer Egypt, the mighty Persian Empire under Darius, and numerous smaller kingdoms along the way. Considered to be one of the great military geniuses of history, the young general was always more interested in fighting and conquering than in actually ruling his people. He died of a fever at the age of thirty-two while he was building a new army for more conquests. Alexander left no organization or appointed leaders for his gigantic empire; on his death, it collapsed (Grant 1964, 61).

- History Chain: Place the following fifteen battle names and dates of Alexander the Great on regular 8½"-✕-11" paper and give them to fifteen students who should hold their name and date cards in front of them and reorder themselves in correct chronological order. Place the following battles of Alexander the Great in their correct chronological order. (Remember that B.C.E.—Before the Current Era—dates go in descending order, not ascending order.)
  1. Persepolis (early 330 B.C.E.) in southern Iran—the capital city of the Persian Empire.
  2. Ancyra (early 333 B.C.E.) in central Turkey, near modern Ankara.
  3. Taxila (326 B.C.E.) on the northernmost Indus River in modern Pakistan, where Alexander's troops mutinied against him and insisted on returning home.
  4. Damascus and Tyre (early 332 B.C.E.) in modern Syria and Lebanon.
  5. Damghan (late 330 B.C.E.) in northern Iran to the south of the Caspian Sea.
  6. Alexandria (late 332 B.C.E.) in Egypt, where he named the major seaport after himself.
  7. Patala (325 B.C.E.) at the mouth of the Indus River in modern Pakistan where the Greek fleet of ships met Alexander and his army on their return home.
  8. Gaulamela (early 331 B.C.E.) in northern Iraq on the upper Tigris River, where Alexander defeated the Persians for a second time.
  9. Babylon (323 B.C.E.) in southern Iraq, where Alexander died of a fever.
  10. Granicus (early 334 B.C.E.), near the current town of Istanbul, Turkey, was Alexander's first major victory.

11. Ephesus (late 334 B.C.E.) on the western shore of modern Turkey.
12. Babylon (late 331 B.C.E.) in modern southern Iraq, the ancient capital of the Mesopotamian Empire.
13. Kabul (329 B.C.E.) in modern Afghanistan.
14. Samarkan (328 B.C.E.) in modern Uzbekistan, the commercial center of the ancient Silk Road to China.
15. Issus (late 333 B.C.E.) in southern Turkey on the modern border with Syria, where Alexander defeated Shah Darius of Persia.

- Map Attack: With a partner in the classroom, a blank world map, and a world atlas, trace the approximate 2,800-mile conquest of Alexander the Great in correct chronological order. Each set of partners should share their map with the other partners in the class to compare their routes. The class in plenary session can then come to a general consensus of the route taken by Alexander the Great and his army between 334 and 323 B.C.E. (Note that the exact locations of many of his battles more than 2,000 years ago are not known, but indicate the approximate locations of these battles from clues given.)

- You Were There: As the talk show host of the popular TV program *You Were There*, interview Alexander the Great (student in costume) to get his spin on why he was such a great military general. Each member of your studio audience should also have at least one question to ask this great general.

- Counter Spin: As the ace reporter of the *Classical Times* newspaper, write up an (imaginary) interview with one or more peoples conquered by Alexander the Great and his army. Be sure to ask them about the devastation, looting, and destruction caused by his army. Do they consider Alexander to be "Great"?

- Obituary: As a major political commentator for *Classical Radio— 323 B.C.E. on your radio dial*, comment on the recent death of Alexander the Great and whether such great generals should be considered heroes or tyrants, who bring only death and sorrow to the world.

- ADV Military Research: Using the library and the Internet for resources, find out about other ancient-era military leaders, such as Thutmose III (circa 1504–1450 B.C.E.) of Egypt, Darius (circa 558–486 B.C.E.) of Persia, Julius Caesar (circa 45 B.C.E.) from Rome, and Trajan (98–117 C.E.), emperor of Rome. From your research, did they take pride in their military achievements or did they eventually regret all the bloodshed they caused? When finished, report your findings to the class.

2.8.0   TRAGEDY AND DISASTER

2.8.1   The Loss of the Library at Alexandria

Some 500,000 of the known manuscripts from the classical world were stored at the Great Library at Alexandria. Some of the manuscripts in this great library were destroyed by one of several fires, some were destroyed by neglect, and Christian iconoclasts destroyed others in their religious fury to eliminate anything not Christian. As a result, we know of only a handful of the 150 or so great Greek writers, and have lost countless thousands of scrolls of classical science, art, and literature (Boorstin 1992, 27).

- Quick Write: Imagine what it must have been like to see the *only* great library in the world burning. In a short paragraph, describe your feelings for everything that was lost in the library. When finished, share your feelings with the class.
- You Were There: As the popular ancient-era TV show host for "You Were There," ask five guests (students in costume) who knew the library in its greatness to comment on its loss. Each member of the studio audience (students in class) should also have a minimum of three questions each to ask the guests.
  1. Zeno Liberius, the former head librarian of the Great Library
  2. Lothus Maximus, a Christian iconoclast
  3. Philonius the Elder, a renowned Greek thinker
  4. Caesar Augustus, who sent his scribes to study at the great library
  5. Cleopatra, who liked to go to the library to read in peace away from her many followers
- ADV What If?: Research the library and the Internet on the contents of the library at Alexandria and then speculate as to how far and how fast world civilization might have progressed had the works of the Great Library at Alexandria remained intact for the scholars of the world to study. Write a short report detailing what you think would have happened to the history of the world as a result. When finished, report your thoughts to the class.

2.9.0 EXPLORATION AND DISCOVERY

2.9.1 Iron and Steel

Iron smelting first took place (circa 4000 B.C.E.) in China and ancient Egypt, but its use spread slowly due to the high temperatures required to melt iron—1,535 degrees Centigrade (2,795 degrees Fahrenheit). Iron was stronger than bronze, easier to find, and there was more of it because it was not dependent on two metals (copper and tin) being found together. China also led the way with a blast furnace (400 B.C.E.) for cast iron and, later, for steel. Early steel was made during classical times in China, India, and Rome, but the process was lost in the West after the fall of Rome in 410 C.E.

- Quick Write: Open an oven when it is 450 degrees Fahrenheit—it's hot! In a short paragraph, describe what it must feel like when opening a blast furnace at 2,795 degrees (more than five times hotter). In your description, be sure to describe what kind of protection you would want to withstand this kind of high temperature needed for iron smelting.
- Bumper Sticker: Create a bumper sticker contrasting the Chinese being able to smelt iron in 4000 B.C.E. and the rest of the world taking thousands of years to achieve this same feat.
- Role Play: Role-play two steelmakers in ancient China describing to a visitor what it is like to be the first steelmakers in the world.
- Action Research: Next time you have a fire in the fireplace or around a campfire, place a piece of iron on the fire and leave it for a time. When you come back, is it glowing red yet? If not, puff a bellows at it to make it hotter. Can you make it hot enough to melt it (2,795 degrees Farenheit) with a bellows? Be safe if you try to do this and do not be disappointed if you fail. (China could melt steel in a blast furnace in 400 B.C.E.; Europe could not do this for another thousand years because they did not know how to get their fires hot enough.)
- ADV Historical Research #1: Using your library and the Internet for resources, make a list of all the Chinese discoveries made long before they were made in Europe and America. Speculate why these discoveries did not take place in Europe and the Americas.
- ADV Historical Research #2: Why did these major Chinese discoveries take so long to reach Europe? What inventions and changes in

history would have greatly speeded up the use of these early Chinese discoveries around the world? Research your library and the Internet to try to find answers to this major historical problem.

2.10.0   INVENTION AND REVOLUTION

2.10.1   Egyptian Hieroglyphics

Egyptian hieroglyphics evolved at an early date (3100 B.C.E.) from pictographs. The ancient Egyptians, like the ancient Mesopotamians, thought that writing came down as a gift from the gods. Illustrated here is simple phonetic translation of several hieroglyphic symbols. You

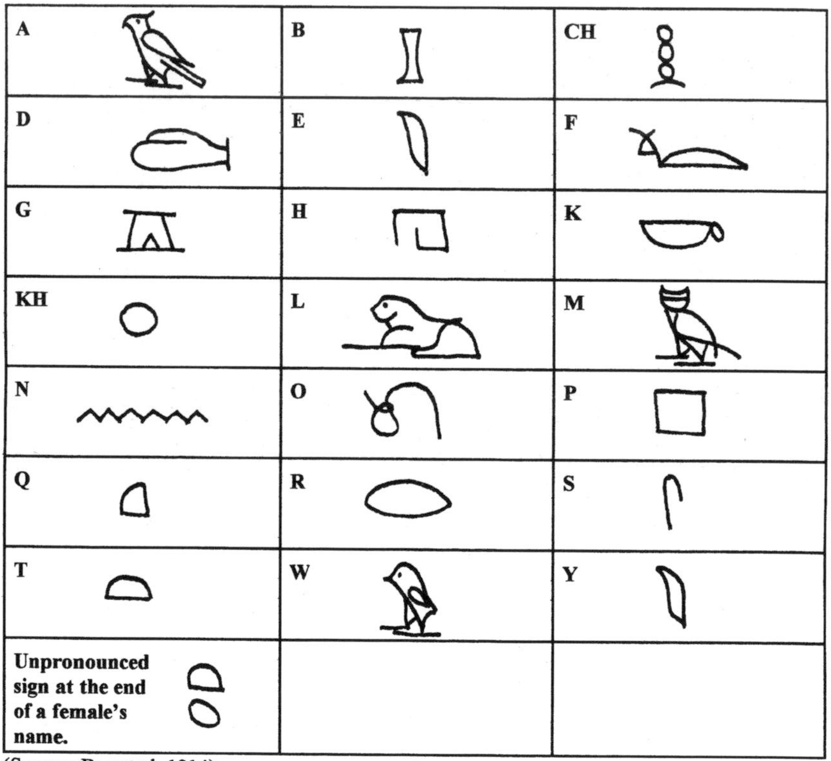

A		B		CH	
D		E		F	
G		H		K	
KH		L		M	
N		O		P	
Q		R		S	
T		W		Y	
Unpronounced sign at the end of a female's name.					

(Source: Breasted, 1914)

Illustration 2.10.1a.   *Phonetical Egyptian Hieroglyphics*

Illustration 2.10.1b. *Ancient Egyptian Cartouche*

might notice that, as with most Middle Eastern languages, hieroglyph-ics did not contain vowel sounds. The circle or cartouche around the group of characters means the word is a name. A half circle at the bot-tom of the cartouche means the person is a female.

- Who Was That Egyptian?: Can you identify the cartouche of this fa-mous ancient Egyptian found in this section? (A cartouche is a round circle with a stand at the end that symbolizes the existence of a name in Egyptian hieroglyphics.) Using the translation of the hieroglyph-ics here, see who can be the first to correctly translate the name of this famous ancient Egyptian in the cartouche. Remember, the name is written in consonants only.
- Write Your Own Name: Now write your own name in hieroglyphics. Remember to encircle it with a cartouche. When finished, exchange

name papers with two classmates—one after the other to mix them up. Have each student then go to the board, eight at a time, to write the hieroglyphic name they have. Who can identify which cartouche belongs to which student in class?

2.10.2   Chinese Writing

Chinese writing also developed at a very early date (circa 1400 B.C.E.) with some 40,000 characters. As with the ancient Egyptians, the ancient Chinese believed that writing was given to them by a divine being. With so many characters, Chinese writing is obviously very hard to learn. Because Chinese characters are independent of pronunciation, these same characters have been adopted by other Chinese dialects (such as Cantonese) and other languages (such as Korean, Japanese, and Vietnamese) to mean very different things in each language.

- Write It: Practice writing the five classical Chinese words. They are translated into English as the words (a) water, (b) word, (c) to be able, (d) river, (e) to criticize.
- Language Analysis: Looking carefully at the five classical Chinese words in illustration 2.10.3, note which words are repeated and appear within other words. They are called "keys" and help us to

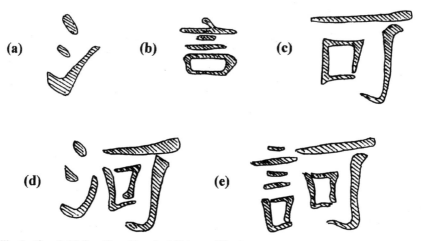

Illustration 2.10.2.   *Five Classical Chinese Words*

understand how the classical Chinese characters were created (Jean 1992, 45).

1. The word "river" in classical Chinese is composed of which two Chinese words?
2. The word "criticize" is composed of which two Chinese words?

- ADV Pronounce it: Learn to pronounce the formal greetings and count from one to five in the following languages. Can any similarity in the languages be noted from how they sound? (Note: The following activities can be done using Microsoft's *Encarta* on CD-ROM, which also has most other major languages in the world.)

1. Mandarin (spoken in the north of China)
2. Cantonese (spoken in the south of China)
3. Korean
4. Japanese
5. Vietnamese

2.10.3 Greek Writing

The Greeks (700 B.C.E.) took the Phoenician phonetic consonants and added vowels to produce an "alphabet" of vowels and consonants together, and they began to write their letters from left to right for some unknown reason.

- Write It: Using the Greek alphabet, write your name in Greek. What changes must take place for you to fully recognize your own name as it is written today in Latin letters?

A	B	G	D	E	Z	Ē	Th	I	K	L	M	N
ΑΒ	ΓΔ	Ε	Ζ	Η	ΘΙ	Κ	Λ	Μ	Ν			

ΑΒ ΓΔ Ε Ζ Η ΘΙ Κ Λ Μ Ν
A   B G D E Z Ē Th I K L M N

Ξ Ο Π Ρ Σ Τ Υ Φ Χ Ψ Ω
Ks O P R S T U Ph Kh Ps O

(See Healy, 1990, p. 39)

Illustration 2.10.3. *Classical Greek Writing*

2.10.4   Do We Need Written Languages?

Why have some written languages failed and others have continued down to our own day? How is our own written language changing? What changes has our language undergone during the past century? What changes will our written language undergo in the future? What specific technological changes in the future will change how we write and how much we write? (For example, consider voice recognition word processors.) What would happen if we lost the ability to write our language?

- Quick Write: Imagine for a moment what it would be like to not have a written language. In a short paragraph, describe what you could do and could not do if you did not have a written language. When finished, share your ideas with the class.
- Bumper Sticker: Create a bumper sticker that promotes the use of written language for those who do not know how to write.
- Poster Power: Create a poster that describes the advantages of written language.
- Quick Skit: With four other student actors from your class, develop and present a short skit demonstrating what it might be like for humankind to lose written language. What would they use in its place?
- The Futurist: Do you think that humankind—with all its rapid technological advances in voice recognition software—could lose its written language in the future? With a classroom partner, develop a presentation that illustrates how this might happen. If so, what would replace written language?
- ADV Linguistic Research #1: Use your library and the Internet to research possible answers why cuneiform in ancient Mesopotamia and hieroglyphics in ancient Egypt did not survive.
- ADV Linguistic Research #2: Using the same sources, try to find out why the Chinese and the Phoenician-based written languages (such as English, Spanish, Greek, and Arabic) survived.
  Research Note: To answer these questions, focus your readings on the advantages and disadvantages of each language. Focus also on who was using the language in each culture. Did everybody use the language or was each language used only for the elite scribes?)
- ADV Linguistic Research #3: Using library and Internet resources, look back at the development of written language. What advantages did written language give to individuals over those who could not

read? What advantages did written language give to the whole development of humanity?

2.10.5 The Wheel

The use of the wheel for carts was invented almost at the same time as a potter's wheel (3500 B.C.E.) in Mesopotamia.

- Quick Write: For a moment, imagine life on our planet Earth without the wheel. Write a short paragraph describing what life might be like without this most important of inventions. When finished, share your ideas with the class.
- Letter to the Editor: Imagine that you are the inventor of the first potter's wheel in the world. Write a letter to the editor of the *Classical Times* newspaper describing your new invention.
- Make a List: Have a competition in class to see who can list the most uses for wheels in one minute.
- Art Mart: Draw a picture of what you think the first wheeled cart might have looked like.
- Working Model: Make a cardboard model of a two-wheeled cart with a wooden or metal axle and moving wheels. Write out a description of the difficulty of making the wheels and axle turn. How did you solve this very basic problem (which was not understood by humans until 3500 B.C.E.)?
- Make a List: Make a list of all the things which would be needed to make wooden wheels and carts run better (for example: better roads, ball bearings, and rubber tires).
- Action Research: Watch a potter make pottery in coils without a wheel, and then make pottery with a potter's wheel.
- ADV Impact Research: Using your library and the Internet for resources, describe the impact of the invention of the wheel on the world and report your findings to the class.

2.11.0 ART AND CREATIVE THOUGHT

2.11.1 Greek Architecture—Perfect Rectangles

The Greeks left us no great pyramid. They left us, however, the style and motif of their architecture (Doric, Ionic, and Corinthian), which we

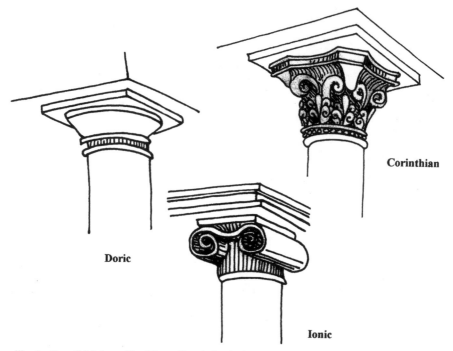

Illustration 2.11.1a.   *The Three Greek Capitals of Ancient Greece*

still copy in our buildings. Although we may admire the size of Greek buildings, it is the beauty of these buildings we love. When we think of Greece, we think of beautiful Greek columns. The tops of these columns (called capitals) tell the history of Greece and give the columns their great beauty. First in history came the Doric capital, with its strong, straight lines; second in history came the Ionic capital, with its curved scrolls; and third came the Corinthian, with its flowering capitals that were copied throughout the Roman Empire.

The Parthenon, the most famous temple in classical Greece, stands in magnificence at the top of the Acropolis in Athens and is a masterpiece of illusion—an illusion of straightness. The vertical columns are not really vertical but sloped inward and upward toward one imaginary point about one mile up, in order to give the illusion of greater height. Each column is also wider in the middle than either the top or bottom to make it appear more massive. The floor gradually slopes away from the center to increase the illusion of size and make sure the rain flowed eas-

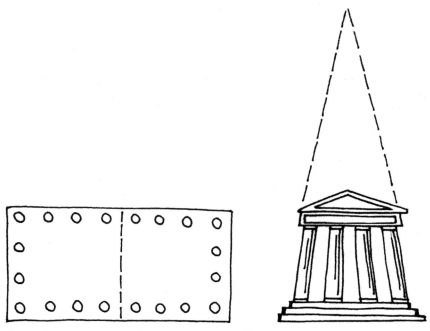

Illustration 2.11.1b.   *The Parthenon at Athens, Greece, circa 432 B.C.E.*

ily away from the temple. These concepts of perspective and illusion in architecture did not appear again in Western art until the Renaissance, another thousand years later.

- Make a Perfect Rectangle: Each Greek temple is a perfect rectangle. Make a square on a piece of paper and double it in one direction. This double square is a "perfect" rectangle and the exact shape of every temple in ancient Greece.
- Comparative Columns: Make a drawing illustrating the differences between the three different types of Greek capitals.
- Interview: Interview three ancient Greek architects (from your class) and have each describe why he or she thinks Doric, Ionic, or Corinthian is the best.
- Model Maker: Make a model of the Parthenon out of clay or cardboard.
- Perspective: Draw a side view of the Parthenon, illustrating the perspective that all of the vertical lines of the columns of the temple will meet about one mile above the Parthenon.

- Poet's Corner: Describe in a poem why the Parthenon has been a symbol of architectural beauty for more than 2,000 years.
- Travel Poster: Make a travel poster for the Greek government advertising the Parthenon.
- ADV Historical Problem #1: Ancient Greek architecture was the same throughout Greece. There was no central Greek state in ancient times. The ancient Greeks did not even have a common Greek language until after the major temples were built. Why do all the Greek temples look the same?

    Historical Note: Later Gothic church architecture during the Middle Ages (500–1300 C.E.) was never uniform and each church was uniquely local in design. Research this question in your library and on the Internet, and report your findings to your class.
- ADV Historical Question #2: We know a lot about Greek architecture today due to Vitruvius, the architect of Julius Caesar (circa 45 B.C.E.). Vitruvius wrote a major work describing Greek architecture in detail. It remained the primary book on architecture for almost 1,500 years. Was it by the accident that his book survived or the greatness of the work that made Vitruvius important?
- ADV Analyze a Quotation: Nietzsche, the famous German thinker, once wrote: "In architecture, the pride of man, his triumph over gravitation, his will to power, assume a visible form." Look at Greek architecture and then explain what Nietzsche meant in this quotation.

2.11.2   Roman Architecture—Cement

The Greeks did not know how to use cement—they used only stone blocks. By the reign of Augustus (63 B.C.E.–13 C.E.), most of the Roman buildings were made out of cement. With cement, the Romans built the world's first true cities, with public administration and public facilities (such as communal public latrines, public baths, and trash collection).

- T Chart: Using a T chart, compare Greek buildings made of stone and Roman buildings made of cement. What advantages did the cement construction have over stone construction?
- What If?: If you were an architect, which would you use in your buildings—stone or cement? Why?

- Action Research: Visit a nearby construction site and watch the builders pour cement. Take notes on your visit and then report to the class on each step builders must take when they are constructing with cement.

2.11.3   Roman Arches and Domes

The mainstay of Roman architecture was the cement brick, from which the Romans were able to construct round structures based on the arch, the vault, and the dome. The Greeks used round architecture only as the arch in their sewers; all classical Greek buildings had to be either square or rectangular in shape, with square mantels above every door and window. The Romans turned round shapes (such as the arch and the dome) into major architectural structures with their cement.

- Poster Power: Make a poster illustrating the basic differences between rectangular classical Greek buildings such as the Parthenon and round classical Roman buildings such as the Pantheon.
- Diorama: Make a diorama illustrating the basic differences between classical Greek and classical Roman buildings side by side.
- Ace Reporter: Write a newspaper article for the *Classical Times* newspaper describing the differences between classical Greek and classical Roman architecture.

2.11.4   Major Historical Problem—Tragedy Sparks Creativity

A great fire in Rome (64 C.E.) destroyed much of the city. Due to this major catastrophe, the eccentric emperor of Rome—named Nero—rebuilt Rome with a frenzy of creative cement works. He also fireproofed much of Rome at the same time. Much of the beauty we see in the remnants of Roman architecture today is the result of Nero's rebuilding efforts.

- ADV Historical Question: Why does tragedy often become the spark that prompts creativity and new ideas? Discuss this question in share pairs, in teams of four, and then in a general class plenary session to share ideas on why this happens in history.

2.11.5   Japanese Architecture

Stonehenge, the pyramids, and the Pantheon were all pieces of great Western architecture. They were built vertically and massively in stone for strength to withstand time and to be a symbol of human dominance over the forces of nature. Japanese architecture is just the opposite in almost every way. Japanese architecture reflects the traditional culture and religion of Japan, which stresses the importance of human submission to the forces of nature. Traditional Japanese temples are low, horizontal, and designed to blend into their natural surroundings (Boorstin 1992).

- Poet Power: Write a small haiku poem that describes in just a few words how traditional Japanese buildings blend with nature.
- Viewpoint: In American society today, old buildings are almost always destroyed to make room for new buildings or parking lots. Compare this with the traditional Japanese view of nature.
- Dialogue: With a partner in the class, write and present a short dialogue between a traditional Japanese architect and a classical Western architect comparing their buildings.
- Personal Preference: In a short essay, explain which type of architecture you prefer (European/American or Japanese) and why you have made this decision.
- ADV Historical Problem: How can two views (European/American and Japanese) of the same thing (architecture) be so different? Research your library and the Internet to try to find the answer to this riddle of major differences between cultures.

2.11.6   Homer's *Iliad* and *Odyssey*

Homer's *Iliad* and *Odyssey* from ancient Greece are among the oldest written works of literature in the world. Educated ancient Greeks were required to memorize *all* of Homer's famous epic tales. Homer's epics were repeated orally for hundreds of years before they were formally written in Greek (circa 700 B.C.E.). A major clue we have to the popularity of the *Iliad* and the *Odyssey* comes from Egypt. Many of the remaining ancient papyri (early paper) scrolls containing Greek writing from late dynastic Egypt are sections from the *Iliad* and the *Odyssey*. Homer's greatness lasted throughout the classical period, the Middle Ages, and the Renaissance into our own day. Homer's stories were about an ancient—even to Homer—Trojan War and the men and women who took part in that war: Achilles, Agamemnon, Helen of Troy, and Odysseus. Homer took no side in the war, but rather tells the tale of superheroes, of regular people confronted by normal problems of love and anger, and the adventures of the very humanlike gods and goddesses. The Greek gods were powerful, but not *all* powerful. They, however, also had weaknesses, made mistakes, and got into trouble, just like human beings. In fact, the Greek gods were patterned after humans. These gods could also be very troublesome to human beings. One-eyed monsters, sirens luring him to his death, giants, and mighty storms all tried to lure Odysseus from his path home in the *Odyssey*.

We do not know who Homer was, but we know that he was a great storyteller, as the following passage from the *Odyssey* illustrates. In the passage, a great blind singer by the name of Demodocus is led to the throne of Pontonoos, King of Phaeacia, to play for the king's banquet. Some scholars think that the passage is a reflection of Homer himself playing for the courts of the early Greek kings (Grant 1964).

Historical Note: The importance of Homer's work cannot be overstated in setting the model for modern literature across Europe, the Middle East, and eventually the world.

The crier soon came, leading that man of song
whom the Muse cherished; by her gift he knew
the good of life, and evil—
for she who lent him sweetness made him blind.
Pontonoos fixed a studded chair for him
hard by a pillar amid the banqueteers,
hanging the taut harp from a peg above him,
and guided up his hands upon the strings.
In time, when hunger and thirst were turned away,
the Must brought to the minstrel's mind a song
of heroes whose great fame rang under heaven.

- Poster Power: Read this passage from the *Odyssey* and illustrate the images the page depicts on a large wall poster.
- Imagine: Imagine the ancient Greek gods depicted in the *Iliad* and the *Odyssey* as being alive today. Draw a picture of what you think they might look like.
- Song Fest: Create an epic song about a modern war and sing it to your class.

- Bumper Sticker: Make a bumper sticker supporting or attacking one of the Greek gods.
- Super Hero: Odysseus is one of the first mythical superheroes we know about in history. Make a list of his major features and then compare him to a modern superhero in a comic book.
- ADV Literary Research: Check out a copy of the *Iliad* and the *Odyssey* from your school library. Read one of the stories, and then report on what it was like to read a book that is almost 3,000 years old.

2.12.0   SUCCESSES AND FAILURES OF THE ANCIENT WORLD

2.12.1   Success or Failure Quiz Show

Success or Failure? This is the competitive quiz show of the ancient era that challenges teams to list as many reasons as possible why a person, place, or thing is the most important success or failure of the classical period.

- Pick a Name: Each student team of four draws the name of a classical person, place, or thing from a hat. The classical names to be used can be as follows or developed from a larger list.

Hatshepsut	cuneiform	the wheel
pyramids	Parthenon	the Pantheon
Moses	Homer	Jesus
cement	Library at Alexandria	Epic of Gilgamesh
Socrates	Alexander the Great	Hammurabi
Akhenaton	Phoenicians	Aristotle
democracy	Great Wall of China	Hinduism
Tao Te Ching	Buddha	Confucius
Linear B	metal making Roman Empire	

- Score Keeper: Each team calls out its name and the scorekeeper puts it on the board as the team's name. The scorekeeper will keep track of how many answers each team gives on the board.
- Make a List: Using any books or materials available, each student team has fifteen minutes to make as long a list as possible of reasons why the name they drew is the most important of the ancient era.

- List Collection: All teams must turn their lists into the scorekeeper at the same time, and the scorekeeper or an assistant may read each list out loud to the class.
- Validators: When each team reports its reasons, the other teams should check to make sure the reasons are correct.
- The Winners: The team with the most number of "valid" supporting reasons wins a free trip to the library.

2.13.0   MAJOR WORLD PROBLEMS FOR THE ANCIENT WORLD

2.13.1   The Problem of Justice—Socrates (469 B.C.E.–399 B.C.E.)

Does individual freedom exist? Can an individual question the religious beliefs of others? Can an individual question the political actions of a state? Can the state impose its will on an individual human being? Does the state have the right to condemn one of its citizens to die? Should an individual willingly die as a martyr in support of his ideals?

These very powerful questions can all be traced back to Socrates—2,400 years ago. Today, these questions still need to be asked. Socrates was a simple scholar who asked questions about people's religious and political beliefs. The people of Athens did not like so many questions and voted to tell him to stop. He refused and they imposed the death penalty on him. Socrates, true to his ideals of free speech and individual liberty, knowingly drank the poison he was given and died.

- Quick Write: People and politicians often do not like to be criticized. In a short paragraph, describe what happens to people today who are very critical of the government. When finished, share your thoughts with the class.
- What If?: Imagine Socrates in your town today. If he asked everybody about their religious and political beliefs—as he did in classical Athens—how popular do you think he would be? What would happen to him?
- Time Travelers: With a partner in class, imagine that you were alive during the time of Socrates in classical Athens. How would you react to Socrates' speeches? What would you do when the people voted to condemn him to death for his views?

- Action Research: The questions of Socrates are some of the most powerful ones we can ask in a democratic society. As a class project, develop a list of Socrates' major questions and make them fit your school and community today. Ask these same questions of students and teachers in your school and of people in your community. What was the response of people to these questions? How did they react?
- Bumper Sticker: Create a bumper sticker either praising or condemning Socrates.
- Action Plan: Develop a community action plan to either support or condemn the ideals of Socrates.
- Class Debate: Socrates died for an ideal. Conduct a debate on whether or not human life is too sacred to die for an ideal.
- Quick Skit: Does the state have the right to impose the death penalty? In pairs, develop a short drama that illustrates Socrates' question of how much power a government has regarding the life and death of an individual. When finished, present it to the class.
- Declaration of Liberty: How far can individual liberty go? Was Socrates right or wrong for questioning religion and the actions of political leaders of the day? In groups of four, write up the formal declarations of individual liberties with which your group would be willing to live.
- Plenary Session: Does the rest of the class agree with the individual liberties of each group? How far can each group express its individual liberties before the whole class tells the group to stop? The class as a whole should discuss these issues.
- ADV Historical Research: Name several other people in history who willingly died for their ideals and compare them to Socrates. Research the library and the Internet for more information on how they died and the cause for which they died. When finished, report your findings to the class.

2.13.2   The Problem of Entropy—The Rise and Fall of the Roman Empire

- ADV Why do great empires (such as the Roman Empire) rise and fall? As an advanced topic of study, here is a list of questions that analyze why great empires fall. In teams of four, carefully read each of the following questions and then carefully read about the rise and fall of Rome from library and Internet sources. From your team's readings and your own thoughts, decide which of the following questions are most important to understand why great empires rise and fall, and report your findings to the class (see Kennedy 1987).

1. Who makes the leadership decisions to direct the empire?
2. How strong are the leaders who make these decisions?
3. Are the leaders willing and able to accept new ideas to improve the empire?
4. Do the leaders have ready sources of new information and new ideas at their disposal?
5. Do the leaders have open communication lines to all parts of the empire?
6. Does the leadership have trusted allies throughout the empire to implement new ideas?
7. What are the central ideas and strengths of the empire?
8. Where is the economic strength of the empire?
9. How secure is this economic strength?
10. Where is the empire using its economic resources?
11. Is the empire using its economic resources to improve itself and grow stronger?
12. Is the leadership of the empire seeking to constantly renew itself and adapt itself to changing conditions?
13. Is the empire spending its economic resources on luxuries rather than on the means of further growth?
14. Has entropy set into the empire with no new ideas, direction, or growth?
15. Is the leadership resistive to new ideas and changes?
16. Has the leadership of the empire lost any sense of direction and is willing to let surrounding events and ideas take their course?
17. Is the leadership not reacting to correct obvious signs of decline in the empire?
18. Has complete entropy and inaction set into the empire as it waits to fall?

- ADV Graph It #1: From your readings and reports on the Roman Empire, create a graph of the major steps in the rise and fall of this great Empire.
- ADV The Futurist: In pairs of students, apply the same questions toward the United States today or any other country in the world. According to your analysis, what stage is this country in—still continuing

to grow or is it in a stage of decline? When finished, present your findings to the class for discussion.

• ADV Graph It #2: From your pair's analysis of the United States, chart the current location of this great country in its rise or fall.

2.14.0   ANCIENT ERA ANTECEDENTS FOR THE FUTURE

2.14.1   Is Humankind Ready to Advance?

It is now time to judge whether or not humankind is ready to advance into the next era. Five members from around the temple grounds (the class) will state their basic viewpoints of whether or not humankind has advanced enough during the ancient era. Should humankind move forward? The five illustrious members are as follows:

1. Lidbit Betrink, the archconservative of the temple, believes that humankind has gone far enough with enough progress. Lidbit believes strongly that the good old days were the best and that humankind needs to hold strongly to past values and beliefs.

2. Makdak Derudzuk, one of the rising young voices at the temple, is a more moderate conservative who believes that we need to be very cautious with any change and be very sure that no harm will come to the temple if change takes place. Makdak is willing to accept some change, but only in very small amounts and only when the time is right—and wants to decide when that time will come.

3. Pitwip Wookbot, the wishy-washy middle-of-the-roader around the temple, is willing to accept change for a few minutes after one speaker, but might have a change of mind in an instant to oppose change after another speaker has finished.

4. Yatsnurk Vatsmeer, the moderate progressive of the group is willing to support change for the good of the people around the temple. Yatsnurk is especially in favor of change that will directly benefit Yatsnurk's own family.

5. Qilmuk Varull, the radical progressive around the temple, is very willing to support any change that will move humanity away from the drafty old Greek temple into something more modern and comfortable for humanity.

• Pick a Position: Each member of the temple community (students) now must chose one of the five positions for humanity to take and support their position with evidence of what they have learned about human beings during the ancient era.

- Plenary Session: A vote will then be taken of all early humans around the temple community to determine whether or not humanity should move on to the next era. The consensus decision of the classic humans around the imaginary temple will determine their own future and the rest of humanity. (In reality, just such decisions by ancient era families were key in deciding whether humans stayed the way they were or progressed to new levels of development.)

The Middle Ages (400 C.E. to 1400 C.E.)

UNIT 3: TABLE OF CONTENTS

INTRODUCTION

The people of the Middle Ages would not have called themselves "middle people." After a moment of contemplation, they might have called themselves "the faithful," for it was an age of faith. All three major monotheistic religions from the great desert of the Middle East, "the People of the Book" (Judaism, Christianity, and Islam) grew into maturity during the Middle Ages. Monotheism, however, does not lend itself to toleration of other religions or even to different interpretations of the same religion. The result was a very long era of bloodshed caused by religious ideology: pogroms, burnings of "heretics," and crusades against unbelievers. Religion, however, was not the only cause of bloodletting during the Middle Ages. Hordes of invaders, from the Huns to the Mongols, swept across Asia and changed the face of Europe, the Middle East, and Asia. The centers of civilization during the Middle Ages were in Christian Constantinople, the Muslim Middle East, and Spain. Scholars in Constantinople passed the learning of the Greeks on to Muslim scholars in Baghdad. This stimulated a major flowering of scientific learning in the Muslim world. Modern medicine, mathematics, and science all can be traced to this Muslim Renaissance (circa 1000 C.E.). Translated by Jewish scholars in Spain and Sicily, this new Muslim science began to flow into Europe. Inspired by these Muslim thinkers, St. Thomas Aquinas (circa 1200 C.E.) paved the way for modern science by insisting that the church be guided by reason and not just faith. This seemingly very small step in theology was a major step during the Middle Ages and led humanity out of the Middle Ages into the Renaissance.

THEMATIC LESSON PACS

3.1.0   HISTORICAL TIME LINE

3.1.1   History Time Line of the Middle Ages

Name Plates: Photocopy six sets of the following thirteen names and items. Cut each name or item into a strip of paper. Place the strips of paper carefully into separate envelopes for each team and label the envelopes "3.1.1 The Middle Ages History Time Line," for later use in class.

- Team Power: Break the class into six teams.
- The Envelope: Each team should be given an envelope containing the following random thirteen names from the Middle Ages era:
  1. The Mongol attack of Baghdad ends the Muslim Renaissance (1258 C.E.).
  2. Charlemagne divides his empire into feudal states (800 C.E.).
  3. Muslim scholars develop modern science, math, and medicine in Baghdad (1000 C.E.).
  4. The Christian crusaders sack Christian Constantinople (1204 C.E.).
  5. Rome is sacked for the first time by the Visigoths (410 C.E.).
  6. Pope Urban II calls for the crusaders to retake the Holy Land from the Muslims (1095 C.E.).
  7. The Byzantine Emperor Justinian develops the world's first law code (483–565 C.E.).
  8. Perhaps the most beautiful piece of architecture in the world— the Alhambra Palace—is built in Granada, Spain (1250 C.E.).
  9. Black Death or Bubonic Plague started in China (1331 C.E.) and wiped out one-third of the world's population.
  10. Muhammad's words from God and written in the Koran become the center of Islam (622 C.E.).
  11. Dante writes *The Divine Comedy*—perhaps the first modern novel (1265 C.E.).
  12. Iconoclasts see all art as sinful and destroy classical statues and paintings (700 C.E.).
  13. The first Gothic cathedral is built in Paris, France (1140 C.E.).
- Team Time Line: The first job of each team is to correctly order the thirteen names and artifacts according to time, with the oldest at the

top and the most recent at the bottom. Each student should separately write the correct time line for the Middle Ages names and artifacts on a personal sheet of paper for later reference.

- Team Look Up: Once every member of the team has a Middle Ages time line on his or her own sheet of paper, each of the thirteen Middle Ages names should be divided between members of the team to find out the meaning of each name from their textbook. Once found, the meanings of each Middle Ages name can be shared with the members of the team to write on their own time lines.
- Poster Power: On a large piece of paper, each team should construct its own time line for the Middle Ages using the thirteen names, with descriptions and illustrations to demonstrate the meaning of each name. When finished, these can be presented to the class and displayed on the classroom wall.
- Music Mart: Each team should pick what they think is the most important name or event in the time line and then compose and present a short song or rap about the name or event. When finished, this can be presented to the class for their approval.
- Journal Entry: Have each team member write a short journal entry speculating about what they now know about the development of humans during the Middle Ages—from the time line they developed—and possibly the most important things to happen during this era. When finished, students can first share their thoughts with their team and then with the class as a whole for general discussion about what they think are the most important things that happened during the era.

3.2.0 SEPARATING FACT FROM MYTH AND PROPAGANDA

3.2.1 The Dark Ages

The period after the fall of the Roman Empire has been called "the Dark Ages," but such a label obviously depends on your point of view. Would the period have been called a "Dark Age" by some of many slaves kept by the Romans or by one of the many peoples conquered by the Romans? By 500 C.E., the lights certainly might have gone out in Rome and most of Europe, but they did not do so in many other areas of the world, such as Constantinople (modern Istanbul in Turkey), Baghdad (in modern Iraq), and in Granada in Muslim Spain. The year 500 C.E. was the beginning of the greatness of the Christian Byzantine

Empire centered in Constantinople. The rise of Islam, and with it the foundations of modern science and mathematics from Baghdad and the artistic and cultural triumphs of Muslim Spain, all took place during the "Dark Ages" of European history.

- Quick Write: In a short paragraph, compare your school with another school. Do they have a better football team? Do they have better dances? Do they have more fun? Is it fair to compare schools without really talking to fellow students from the other school?
- Map Attack: Using an atlas and a blank map of Europe and the Middle East, locate Rome (the former great capital of the Roman Empire), Constantinople (the capital of the Byzantine Empire), Baghdad (the early capital of the Muslim world), and Granada (one of the cultural centers of Muslim Spain).
- Cartoonist: Draw a comical cartoon of a poor European during the "Dark Ages" of Europe looking longingly at the splendors of Baghdad at the same time period of history.
- ADV Bias Detector: What does the use of such terms as the "Dark Ages" tell us about the bias of the writers who use the term? What would Byzantine and Muslim writers from about 1000 C.E. have thought of the term the "Dark Ages" to describe the era in which they lived?

3.2.2   The P.R. Spin of Attila the Hun (circa 451 C.E.)

Attila, during the last days of the Roman Empire, had an excellent P.R. (public relations) team, who spread terror among the citizens of the Roman Empire. One such tale was that the Huns "roasted pregnant women alive, ate the flesh of children, and drank the blood of women." The potential enemies of the Huns, including the city of Rome itself, believed such tales and bribed Attila with huge sums of gold and silver not to attack them (Mee 1993, 22).

- Spin Doctor: As one of Attila the Hun's advance team, create a wild and bloodthirsty rumor about Attila that would terrorize towns into paying huge bribes to Attila.
- Counter Spin: The students in your class are now an imaginary town in northern Italy threatened to be attacked by Attila the Hun. Develop a counter P.R. story about your town that might convince Attila not to attack your town.

- Contingency Plan: In case your counter P.R. plan against Attila the Hun does not work, develop a contingency plan to deal with this awesome enemy. Will you bribe him, fight him, or flee? Explain your response using a decision tree.

3.3.0 LOCATION AND MOVEMENT

3.3.1 Global Climate Fluctuations (circa 350–450 C.E.)

For one hundred years or more, a major drought in central Asia (circa 350–450 C.E.) forced the herding people of that region south and west into Europe. The Huns from north of the Aral Sea were the first to feel the effects of the drought. They moved into Russia (355 C.E.) and then across the Volga River (circa 372 C.E.) to attack the Ostrogoths and the Visigoths. The Ostrogoths and Visigoths then fled into the very weak Roman Empire, followed by the Huns under Attila in 451 C.E. These invasions crushed the empty shell of what remained of the former Roman Empire.

- Quick Write: Write a short paragraph about what would happen if our planet Earth suddenly became much colder and dryer. How would this affect your life?
- Map Attack: Using an atlas and a blank map of Europe and the Middle East, trace the early movement of the Huns across Europe into the Roman Empire before 451 C.E. from the preceding description.
- What If?: In a pair share, talk with a partner in class for one minute each about what you would do if you were a citizen of classic Rome and you saw 300,000 mounted Huns on horseback coming swiftly toward your town. When finished, share your feelings with the class.
- ADV Climate Doctor: Look for books and articles in your library on climatic change and how climatic change has affected human history. Report to your class on your findings.
- ADV Climate Doctor (today): Read about the possibilities of climatic change today. How would such a climatic change directly affect you today? What if the world suddenly became warmer? What if it suddenly became colder? How would such climatic changes affect how we live on Earth? How would humans react to these changes? Develop a short presentation to the class on your findings.
- ADV Climate Doctor (tomorrow): In teams of four, each team should develop two strategies for coping with climate—one for developing

a plan for all humanity to adjust to the impact of global warming on the world, the other for humanity to adjust to global cooling and perhaps a new Ice Age. When finished, each team should present its strategies to all the gathered people of the Middle Ages (your class) for their deliberation.

3.3.2   The Kaaba—The Holy Stone of Islam

Since the earliest times, large stones have played a major part in the history of the Middle East. One of the most important of these is the Kaaba in Mecca, based on Psalm 118:22–23: "The stone which the builders rejected has become the head of the corner: This is God's doing." In the corner of the large square of the Kaaba is a small meteorite, which Muslims consider to be this very stone placed there by God. This is the holiest spot for all Muslims.

- Map Work: On a map, locate Mecca in the current country of Saudi Arabia.
- Travel Planner: Once a lifetime, Muslims are to pay a visit to Mecca to worship at the Kaaba—this pilgrimage is called the "hajj." As the imaginary travel agent of a Muslim family of six, plan all of the details of the family's trip to Mecca:
  1. The total air mileage of the trip from your town to Mecca and return.
  2. The route you will have the family travel to Mecca and back.
  3. The total cost of the trip. Call a major international airline to get the exact air fare.
  4. Present your final trip plans to your class.

3.3.3   The Dome of the Rock

More humans have died fighting for control of the Dome of the Rock in Jerusalem than any place on Earth—and it remains so today. All three desert religions—Judaism, Christianity, and Islam—consider this rock sacred. Four major religious traditions surround this rock: God prevented Abraham from killing his son at this rock (symbolic for ending human sacrifice), the prophet Elijah rose to heaven from this rock, Jesus died on the cross a few hundred yards from this holy rock, and the prophet Mohammed rose to heaven from the Dome of the Rock.

- Map Work: Find Jerusalem on a map.
- Poster Power: Draw a poster illustrating why Judaism, Christianity, and Islam all consider Jerusalem to be holy.
- U.N. Mediator: As an imaginary United Nations command team, develop a plan for all three religions to stop fighting over the area of Jerusalem surrounding the Dome of the Rock.
- ADV Web Master: Find Web sites and newspaper articles on Jerusalem. What is the current relationship between these three major religions in the city of Jerusalem?

3.3.4 Constantinople—The Thousand-Year Point Guard

European history books never give enough credit to Constantinople and the Byzantine Empire. Between 453 C.E. and 1453 C.E., Constantinople ran interference for Europe from any number of possible invaders from the East. The history of Europe and Christianity would have been much different if the massive armies of Islam had swept across a powerless Europe during the Middle Ages. Any such Muslim thoughts of invading Europe were stopped at Constantinople for a thousand years. In the reverse direction, during each of the Crusades, the crusaders from Western Europe used Constantinople as the staging point for their attacks against the Muslims in Palestine.

- Map Attack: Look on a map of the world and determine why Constantinople (modern Istanbul) is in such a crucial location in the world in terms of East vs. West relations. In a short paragraph, report your conclusions to the class.
- What If?: In a hypothetical scenario, remove Constantinople and the Byzantine Empire from the history books between 453 C.E. and 1453 C.E. Using a large map, plot the likely invasion route of the Muslim armies into Europe.
- Skit Builder: Create a short skit (a "trilogue," meaning with three people) and present it to your class between a crusader from France, a Byzantine soldier in Constantinople, and a Muslim soldier under Saladin discussing whether or not the crusaders could have attacked the Muslims in Palestine without the assistance of Constantinople.
- ADV T Chart: Would early Christianity in western Europe be able to survive a large Muslim invasion without the assistance of Constantinople? Using your library and the Internet as sources, compare both

the pros and the cons of such a possibility on a T chart and present it to your class.

3.3.5   Mansa Musa's Gold (1324 C.E.)

Mansa Musa, the king of Mali (1312–1340) in West Africa, set off on a simple pilgrimage to Mecca in 1324. His trip followed the trade routes across the Sahara Desert to North Africa and then east across North Africa through Cairo in Egypt to Mecca. What Mansa Musa did on his trip, however, had repercussions far into the future. He paid for everything he needed with gold. Lots of gold. Never had the world seen a man with so much gold. How could one man have so much gold? Where did he get it? Mansa Musa's gold set men's eyes aflame with dreams of piles of gold. Somewhere in West Africa, across the Sahara Desert, beyond Timbuktu, was Mansa Musa's immense source of gold. It became the dream of nations to find this source of gold (Ajayi and Espie 1965).

Note from the Future: Portugal's Prince Henry the Navigator would turn this dream of Mansa Musa's gold into reality and begin Europe's age of exploration during the fifteenth century. It began with Mansa Musa's pilgrimage to Mecca.

- Map Attack: On a blank map of Africa and the Middle East, trace the route of Mansa Musa's trip to Mecca.
- Newspaper Reporter: As the star reporter for the *Medieval Times* newspaper, interview people in Egypt (students) who witnessed Mansa Musa's lavish display of gold. Write an article on your interviews for the next edition of the newspaper.
- The Gold Bug Adventure Company: As a group of four adventurers (students), form a company starting from Fez, Morocco, and make a plan to travel to Timbuktu in Mali, West Africa, to locate and acquire some of Mansa Musa's gold. Do take into consideration, however, that a trip across the Sahara takes 114 days by camel and that large protection fees need to be paid to Tuareg guides. Ships capable of rounding West Africa and compasses to point the way are not yet in general use in Europe.

  Your Gold Bug plan must include the following:
  1. A map of how you plan to get there
  2. Your means of transportation
  3. Your method of acquiring the gold

Present your plan to the class. The class, in turn, will rate the possibility of your company's success on a 1–5 scale (where 5 means excellent and 1 means you are very unlikely to succeed). Good luck, Gold Bugs.

3.3.6   Square Towns or Natural Towns

Empires based on military strength, such as the Romans, built their towns in square blocks with straight streets to facilitate rapid troop movement. Most ancient nonmilitary towns of the world (such as Fez,

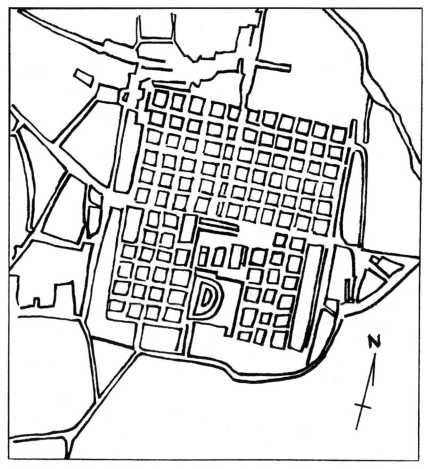

Illustration 3.3.6a.   Sketch of an Aerial View of a "Square" Roman Town Timgad, Algeria circa 100 C.E.

Morocco, or Toledo, Spain), however, were natural towns with roads, houses, and buildings following a natural randomness of crooked little streets and not perfectly symmetrical buildings. With the collapse of the Roman Empire, the towns of Europe gradually returned to this nat-

Illustration 3.3.6b.   *A Natural Town and its twisty little streets, Isle of Rhodes, circa 1200 C.E.*

ural form of town with the crooked little streets that we see in many old European towns today.

- Map Attack: Make two maps—one of an imaginary natural town with crooked streets, and one of an imaginary town with straight streets and square blocks. Which type of town do you prefer and why?
- Letter Writer: Imagine living in such an old natural town with tight little crooked streets and houses close together. Write a letter to an imaginary friend describing what it would be like living in such a town.
- Town Planner: Why are most of the towns laid out in square blocks and straight streets in the United States? Why are there very few towns in the United States with crooked little streets and houses? Why are some modern suburbs becoming more natural with circular rather than straight roads?
- Town Planner II: Why do many people around the world like to live in natural towns when there is no strong government telling them to make straight streets and square houses?
- Field Work: Interview someone who has either visited or lived in a natural town with crooked little streets and packed together houses. Which type of town do they prefer? Why do they prefer one type of town to the other?
- ADV Photo Analysis: Go to the library to try to find pictures of old natural towns of the world, such as Fez, Morocco, or Toledo, Spain, to see all the crooked streets and houses packed tightly together. How are these cities different from your hometown? Why do you think they are so different? When finished, report your findings to the class.

3.4.0   POLITICS AND LEADERSHIP

3.4.1   The Collapse of Rome (410–455 C.E.)

The huge border of the Roman Empire was 10,000 miles long in 410 C.E. and had very few soldiers to defend it. The Romans had no new ideas to counter the economic and social decline. Roman armies no longer stole treasures from other lands to run the economy of Rome. Gothic (German) slaves and soldiers now did most of the work in

Rome and guarded the borders. The Roman Empire was a shell ready to break; it had declined into entropy disorder. The population of the city of Rome fell to one-sixth its former size—from 1.5 million to 300,000 people. With the attacks from the Visigoths (410 C.E.), the Huns (451 C.E.), and the Vandals (455 C.E.), the greatness and riches of Rome were no more (Durant 1950, 35–43).

- Song Writer: Create a ballad or rap song telling the tale of the fall of Rome.
- Poster Power: Pick a side and then create a poster either defending the Roman Empire or supporting its demise.
- You Were There: Create a panel of expert witnesses (from the class) to analyze the fall of Rome. The witnesses should come dressed to fit the part, and members of the class should each have a minimum of three challenging questions to ask the witnesses about the fall of Rome. This list of witnesses should include such illuminati as:
  1. Attila the Hun, who leveled northern Italy in 451 C.E.
  2. Placidia, the Roman wife of Aleric, whose Visigoths sacked Rome in 410 C.E.
  3. Albertus, a Roman slave from Germany, who joined the Visigothic sack of Rome in 410 C.E.
  4. Licretius, the wife of a wealthy Roman Senator who fled Rome during the "barbarian" attacks.
  5. Leo III, the Catholic pope in Rome, who convinced Attila not to attack Rome in 451 C.E.
- ADV Why Did It Happen?: Research sources on the fall of Rome in your library, such as Durant (1950) and on the Internet, and then make up your own list of reasons why you think the Roman Empire fell.
- ADV The Futurist: With a partner from the class, discuss briefly what lessons countries, such as the United States, can learn from the fall of Rome, and then share your ideas with the class for their consideration and conclusions.

3.4.2   Justinian (483–565 C.E.)

From their capital at Constantinople, the Byzantines, under the command of Justinian and his wife, Theodora, reestablished rule over the eastern Roman Empire after the fall of Rome. Justinian's major contribution, however, was the written codification of Roman law. Before his rule, the Byzantines were buried in lawsuits by unscrupulous lawyers. Justinian's codification cut down on the frivolous litigation, became the one law code of all of Europe, and had no competition for 1,300 years.

- Map Attack: Locate Constantinople on a map (modern Istanbul in Turkey). Determine the following:
  1. How far in miles and kilometers it is from your home?
  2. How long will it take to travel there by air traveling at 500 miles an hour?
  3. How long would it have taken to travel there by horse and boat traveling there during the Middle Ages at fifty miles a day?
- Quick Write: Think for a moment and then describe a law you would like to see enacted. Imagine what your law would look like 1,300 years later.
- Pair Share: Share your law with your partner.
- Room Share: Share your laws with the class. As a class, decide which laws you like best and which might last 1,300 years—as Justinian's Law Code did.
- ADV Historical Research: Using your library and the Internet, read about the law code of Justinian and its impact on our law codes today. When finished, report your findings to the class.

3.4.3   Charlemagne and Feudalism (800 C.E.)

There was not much of Europe in 800 C.E. The Roman Empire was long gone and even the fifth-century invaders who toppled Rome were either gone or had settled down. Only one man had big ideas in 800 C.E. Europe—Charlemagne (Charles the Magnificent). With very little opposition, he conquered most of western Europe and declared it the Holy Roman Empire. Although a good fighter, he did not know how to read or write, and he knew he did not have the power to hold his empire together for long. He solved this problem by giving land and people to his loyal vassals to rule in his name. Each vassal, in turn, would pay a yearly tribute or tax to him in soldiers, servants, sheep, or grain. In so doing, Charlemagne accidentally created a "feudal" system of rule that would dominate how most of Europe would be ruled for almost 500 years—until the Black Death during the thirteenth century.

- Quick Write: If you were king or queen of your school, write a short paragraph describing how you would rule your kingdom. Are you strong enough to rule the kingdom by yourself? If not, which of your friends would you have help you to rule, and which areas of the kingdom would you have them rule?
- Time Machine: If you were king or queen of an imaginary feudal state of Morania during the Middle Ages, describe the feudal organization of your realm. Who were your vassals? What kind of tribute did they pay to you? Where was your castle? How many knights did you have? How many peasants and serfs worked your fields?
- Map Attack: Draw a map of your imaginary feudal kingdom of Morania indicating your castle, the feudal lands held by your vassals, where the peasants and serfs lived, and the lands they toiled in your service.
- Model Maker: Create a three-dimensional diorama of your castle in the feudal kingdom of Morania. Label all the important parts of the castle—moat, keep, drawbridge, and living quarters. Also label where serfs and peasants lived and worked.
- What If?: What if you were a serf in the feudal kingdom of Morania, toiling in the fields of the king? What aspirations would you have as a serf? Would you ever hope to be anything other than a serf? How would you improve yourself? What if the king opposed the idea of your improving yourself? What would you do? Write a description of what it would be like to be a serf, and what you would change if you were a serf. When finished, present your ideas to the class.
- ADV Historical Research: Using resources in your library and on the Internet, examine Charlemagne's life and how he attempted to rule Europe through "feudalism." In a short research paper, describe whether you think he was successful or not, and report your findings to the class.

3.4.4 *Magna Carta* (1215 C.E.)

The first successful rebellion against feudalism was by the vassals of King John of England in 1215 C.E. At sword point, the vassals forced him to sign a paper called the *Magna Carta,* which guaranteed their rights against unjust actions by the king. This was the first time in history that people demanded that they could stop actions of the king they did not like.

Note from the Future: The *Magna Carta* became the first step in what we now call human rights against the arbitrary rules of kings and governments.

- Quick Right: Which, in your view, is the most important human right we have? Write a paragraph describing your view.
- Create a Skit: Develop a skit with four members of your class demonstrating the forced signing of the *Magna Carta* by King John.
- Newspaper Reporter: As a reporter for the *Medieval Times* newspaper, write a front-page headline story about the signing of the *Magna Carta*.
- What If?: What if Thomas Jefferson, one of founders of the concept of human rights in 1776, traveled back in time to be with the vassals and King John in 1215? What would he say to King John? What would he say to the vassals?

3.5.0   SOCIAL AND ECONOMIC LIFE

3.5.1   Theodora, Empress of Byzantium (483–565 C.E.)

Justinian was a wimp! He might have been the greatest Byzantine emperor in history, but whenever the going got tough, Theodora, his wife, was there to push him on to crush rebellions, build one of the major churches in the world (the Hagia Sophia), and to codify Roman law. In turn, Theodora, daughter of a lion tamer, empress of the Byzantine Empire, became one of the most powerful women in history (see Severy 1983).

- Gossip Column: Make up a ridiculous story for the *Medieval Times* newspaper of how a lion tamer's daughter became one of the most powerful women in history and completely controlled her husband, the emperor. (The problem with this story, however, is that it was true!).
- Bumper Sticker: Create an appropriate bumper sticker for Theodora to stick on the back of her human-drawn carriage.
- Time Travelers: With a partner, go back to the Byzantine Empire in 560 C.E. You have been granted an audience with Empress Theodora. Make a list of questions you plan to ask her and present a list of answers you think she will give to your questions.

- Quick Skit: With a team of four student actors from the class, create a short skit that illustrates how Theodora and Justinian might have ruled the Byzantine Empire together.
- ADV Rank Them: After searching the library and the Internet, who do you think are the three most important women in history? Rank them in order of their importance and describe why you think they are important. When finished, report your findings to the class.

3.5.2   Education during the Middle Ages

Early Christian leaders such as Pope Gregory I (circa 540–604 C.E.) believed that the general public—both children and adults—should *not* be educated. These early leaders of Christianity believed that people, if they knew how to read and write, might read things that were anti-Christian. These early church leaders believed that education was only for the priests so that they could read and write about their God. Under this religious system, only the priests would have access to the word of God, and the people would have to come to the priests to hear the word of God or be sent to hell. The result, during the Middle Ages, was that the general public was uneducated, and the priests had a monopoly of access to the Christian God, as well as a near-monopoly on education, including such basics as reading and writing (Boorstin 1992, 245).

- T Chart: With a T chart, list the advantages and disadvantages the early church gained by having only the priests read or write, and an entire population of people who could not read or write.
- Time Traveler: Imagine Pope Gregory I visiting the United States today. What would he say about the educational system for everyone? Write a speech for the pope concerning education in this country.
- Quick Skit: Write and present a short skit with four student actors from your village (the classroom) discussing education in Europe during the Middle Ages. The four imaginary people are as follows:
  1. Magdalena—a devote, illiterate churchgoer who faithfully follows what the local priest tells her to do
  2. Giotto (Joseph)—the local Christian priest
  3. Johannis—a servant boy who wants to learn how to read and write
  4. Heloise—the daughter of a local wealthy merchant who secretly learned how to read and write

- ADV Amicus Curiae: As an imaginary trusted advisor to the pope during the Middle Ages, write a position paper (amicus curiae) outlining the directions in education you think the church should take.

3.5.3 Eleanor of Aquitaine

She has been called "a bad wife," "a bad mother," and "a bad queen"— and also "Wow, what a woman!" Eleanor of Aquitaine (1122–1204) was born in a man's world, but became one of the great women of history by marrying the kings of both France and England. It is certain that her first husband, the boring King Louis VII of France, wished that she had stayed at home and knitted while he was off fighting the Second Crusade (1147) in Palestine; instead, she followed his French army into battle with her own entourage of ladies-in-waiting and troubadours. Bored with Louis, she convinced the pope to accept a divorce between them, and then married the future king of England, Henry II. Both Eleanor and the younger Henry had hot tempers and passionate beliefs, and clashed about everything. Fed up with his high-strung queen, Henry finally confined Eleanor to house arrest for sixteen years so he could rule England by himself. Troubadours sang with sorrow over poor Eleanor, and their sons fought to dethrone their father and free their mother, Eleanor. When Henry died in 1189, their son Richard the Lionhearted became king and freed his mother to become Regent of England while he was off to fight the Third Crusade against Saladin. When her other son Richard became king, she retired to a convent in France, where she died at the age of eighty-two (Durant 1950).

- Quick Write: In a short paragraph, imagine what it would be like to meet a woman who went off to help fight in a foreign war and then marry the kings of two different countries. When finished, share your thoughts with the class.
- Rump Sticker: Create an appropriate rump sticker to place on the back of Eleanor of Aquitaine's horse.
- Poster Power: Create a poster that illustrates the extraordinary life of Eleanor of Aquitaine.
- Medieval Gossip Columnist: As an imaginary gossip columnist for the *Medieval Times* newspaper, write an ever-so-revealing column from unnamed sources about the simply scandalous behavior of

Eleanor of Aquitaine. Why won't she just stay at home in the kitchen raising children?

- Front Page: With a team of reporters (students from the class) from the *Medieval Times* newspaper, create a front-page edition focused on an exclusive interview with Eleanor of Aquitaine. Be sure to add a drawing of what she might have look like as well as a discussion about her marriages to two kings and going on the Crusades.
- Women's Liberation: Women's liberation is a recent phenomenon, but Eleanor of Aquitaine from the Middle Ages certainly fits the model. Imagine Eleanor of Aquitaine visiting your hometown today. Discuss with a partner what you think she would tell the students in your school, and then share these ideas with your class.
- ADV Historical Comparison: Using the resources in your library and on the Internet, look for other women in history and compare them to Eleanor of Aquitaine. When finished, present your findings to the class.

3.5.4   How About Some Medieval Pollution!

Many of the people of Europe during the Middle Ages lived in walled towns for protection—but these towns did not have any toilets, sewers, or garbage collection services. People dumped their human waste and garbage out the window into the street or river. The pigs, chickens, and fish then ate the human waste and garbage—and guess who ate the pigs, chickens, and fish? When the streets became so bad nobody could walk in them, everybody would dump the human waste and garbage over the city wall. Piles of human waste and garbage then accumulated for years on the outside of the city walls. During the Middle Ages, many towns were defeated in battle because the enemy was able to walk up the piles of human waste and garbage and easily climb over the city wall and capture the city (Durant 1950).

- Quick Write: In a short paragraph, quickly describe the sight and smell of a pile of old garbage and human waste.
- Time Travelers: With a classroom partner, imagine you are visitors to a town during the Middle Ages, and describe to each other the sights and smells of pollution you witness.
- Poster Power: Create a poster that illustrates the major pollution problems of cities during the Middle Ages.

- Bumper Sticker: Create a bumper sticker for wagons during the Middle Ages to encourage people to dispose of their garbage and human waste outside of town.
- Citizen's Action Council: As the Citizen's Action Council of four students representing a neighborhood of a small city during the Middle Ages, what rules would you make regarding pollution? How would you ensure that your policies were implemented?
- Town Council: When the Citizen's Action Councils representing each neighborhood are finished, the Town Council (the whole class) can meet to see what actions can be taken regarding cleaning the town's immense pollution problems during the Middle Ages.
- ADV Comparative Research: Using your local library and the Internet, compare the pollution problems in your own town to the pollution problems during the Middle Ages.

3.5.5   Medieval Cleanliness

Whoever said "Cleanliness is next to godliness" did not live during the early years of Christianity. The ancient Romans were very fond of their daily baths, but anything the ancient Romans did, the early Christians saw as evil—including bathing. Early Christians also had a major model of an unwashed holy man in James, the brother of Jesus—who never washed or cut his hair (Josephus 1988). As a result, the early Christians throughout Europe saw bathing as sinful. An average person on the street might take a bath only once or twice a lifetime. The idea of taking baths reentered Europe with the crusaders who rather enjoyed the old Roman/Turkish baths they found in Constantinople and the Middle East. As late as 1588, however, bathing was still not very popular in Europe. In that year, Queen Elizabeth I of England issued a rule that required that members of her royal court take baths at least once a year—whether they liked it or not. Royalty during the late Middle Ages began to add perfume to each article of clothing to counter their own body odors.

Historical Note: We can only imagine today—with horror—the smells of a crowded room during the Middle Ages.

- Quick Write: In a short paragraph, describe the smell of someone who has not taken a bath in several days.
- Poet's Corner: Create a poem or song about the rather strong smells of the Middle Ages.

- Pro or Con: Take the position of an early Christian during the Middle Ages and create an argument either that bathing is unnatural and against the will of God or that "cleanliness is next to godliness."
- What If?: If you had to live during the Middle Ages, what steps would you take to ensure the survival of your nose?
- Role Play: If you were a king or queen during the Middle Ages, what requirements of cleanliness would you require for your subjects? What penalties would you establish for subjects who disobeyed you?

3.5.6   Ye Olde Medieval Faire

- ADV Middle Ages Recreation: Attend a Medieval Faire in your area or put one on for your school. Everyone must dress up for the faire as faire maidens, knights, nobles, peasants, and perhaps even a medieval dragon or two. Be sure to have grog (punch) to drink, archery contests, medieval music on CD, and a drama based on the Middle Ages.

3.6.0   RELIGIOUS THOUGHT

3.6.1   A Church Meeting in Nicaea (325 C.E.)

The meeting of Church leaders in Nicaea (in modern Turkey) in 325 C.E. had a major argument on its hands—Who was Jesus? Was he God or was he human? There were many different views of Jesus:

1. Was he a Jewish political/religious rebel and "king of the Jews" who sought to overthrow the Roman rule of Judea? This was certainly the view of the Romans and likely the reason for his execution (circa 30 C.E.).
2. Was he the promised political/religious Messiah (savior) of the Jews who was not God—but who rose to heaven, as had Moses and Elijah? This was the view of James, the brother of Jesus, the disciples, and the early Jewish Christians (circa 40–70 C.E.).
3. Was he a man whom God raised from the dead to become the Son of God? This was the view of St. Paul, an early Christian leader (see Romans 1:1–10 and Galicians 1:1–10), circa 50 C.E.

4. Was he a follower of John the Baptist who was made the Son of God by the Holy Spirit when he was baptized? This was the view of St. Mark (see Mark 1:9–11), an early Christian writer (circa 60 C.E.).
5. Was Jesus the word of God from the beginning of time who came down from heaven to become human for a short time before returning to heaven? This was the view of John (see John 1:1–18), an early Christian writer (circa 120 C.E.).
6. Was he the highest level of human, but not God? This was taught by the Egyptian Christian priest named Arius (circa 318 C.E.) and his followers called Arians.

To resolve these differences, the Roman Emperor Constantine called all the Christian leaders to the town of Nicaea (in 325 C.E.) for a church council to decide on the relationship between Jesus and God.

- Time Machine: Your whole class has now boarded a time machine back to that famous Council of Nicaea in 325 C.E.
- Time Warp: Wait a moment for everyone to get over their sense of time warp—it can be very dizzying at times.
- Role Play: The teacher is now the Emperor Constantine and the class is divided into six groups each representing one of the above six positions.
  1. Each student should now stop and think about the position they are about to take. In a quick write, describe one or more reasons for supporting this position.
  2. Each group should then get together to develop an argument in front of the class for their position.
  3. Each group of "church leaders" should then present their argument in front of the Council of Nicaea (the class).
  4. The Council should then vote to determine what beliefs Christians should have about Jesus and God.
  5. The vote of the class Council of Nicaea can then be compared with the real Council of Nicaea of 325 c.e. (see below).

Historical Note: The Council voted 318 to 5 in favor of a Nicene Creed, which saw the Christian God as a three-in-one trinity of the Father, Son, and Holy Ghost. The bishops attending the meeting were mostly from Asia. Most western European, Roman, and Egyptian bishops supporting other views either were not interested in this theological argument and did not come, or were not able to make the Council meeting (see Durant 1950, 658–660).

3.6.2   The Real Beginning of the Middle Ages

The Council of Nicaea (325 C.E.) was the real beginning of the Middle Ages. Christianity was rapidly growing and old Greek and Roman gods were disappearing. The religious leaders of Christianity were also confident enough of their growing power to become intolerant of different ways of belief. The council decided that all other Christian teachings should be burned and teachers of other doctrines killed. The classical Greek and Roman belief in reason was rapidly being replaced by faith in religious ideas (Durant 1950, 658–660).

- Quick Write: The word "intolerance" is an important word to understand. Try to define it and give an example from your own personal experience.
- Concept Web: The class can compare their examples of intolerance using a Concept Web on the board.
- Role Play: The class should be divided into five groups: snow boarders, skiers, in-line skaters, skate boarders, and couch potatoes.
  1. Each of the five groups should make its list of intolerant demands to try to impose its belief on the others.
  2. Each group should also state which penalties should be imposed on other groups.
  3. The intolerant demands and penalties of each group can then be presented to the class.
  4. The class, as a whole, should then examine these intolerant demands and come to an agreement on how to resolve the differences of belief between these groups.
  5. In a concluding essay, each student should describe his or her personal experience with intolerance and make suggestions on how it should be stopped across the world.

3.6.3   Faith versus Reason—The Real Battle of the Middle Ages

St. Augustine (354–430 C.E.) set the transition point between the era of classical Greece and Rome and the following Middle Ages, which he described as the difference between reason and faith. He taught that goodness did not come from humans but from God. To Augustine, "reason" and "bodily pleasure" were evil. If left alone, said Augustine, the "free will" of humans would lead them to evil. The only way humans could become free of evil, said Augustine, was by a faith in God—and faith in God was given to humans only by the grace of God.

The teachings of Augustine ended a thousand years of Greek and Roman belief in the supremacy of reason. With Augustine, western Europe rejected the ideas of great thinkers from ancient Greece and Rome, such as Aristotle and Plato, and put its faith in the new Christian God. The importance of reason would not reemerge for almost another thousand years in western Europe. The same argument between faith and reason also took place during the Middle Ages within Judaism and within Islam.

Note from the Future: The beginnings of the Renaissance (unit 4) during the fourteenth and fifteenth centuries are in large part a revival of the classical Greek and Roman trust in reason. The Augustinian position of the supremacy of faith over reason, however, reappears in the early sixteenth century in the Protestant Reformation of Martin Luther (Durant 1950, 64–79).

- Quick Write: In a personal statement that you do not have to reveal to anyone, write down whether your basic trust is in faith or reason.
- Bumper Sticker: If St. Augustine needed a bumper sticker, what do you think it would say?
- Ace Reporter: As the ace reporter from the *Medieval Times* newspaper, go back in time to interview St. Augustine concerning his views on reason and faith. Write up your interview as a newspaper feature article for the front page.
- Roman Rebuttal: As a former Roman senator from an old and noble family, write a rebuttal to St. Augustine's belief that faith is more important than reason, to be published in the next edition of the *Medieval Times*.
- Editorial: The *Medieval Times* newspaper has asked you to write an editorial defending either the importance of faith or the importance of reason.
- ADV Research Essay: Compare the battle between faith and reason during the early Middle Ages with the same battle today with issues such as abortion rights.

3.6.4   The East/West Split (circa 730 C.E.)

By 700 C.E., with the iconoclastic movement in full swing, many Christians in western Europe began to follow and believe in another Biblical passage (Genesis 1:27): "God created man in his own image." These Christians in western Europe started making statues and paintings of Jesus to "see the image of God." The Byzantine Emperor Leo III (717–741 C.E.) in Constantinople was enraged to think of Christians making statues and paintings and began to destroy as many of such images as he could find. The Western churches, led by the pope in Rome, strongly opposed Leo III's destruction of Christian art. This friction over the meaning of two biblical verses was the beginning of the long split between the Eastern Orthodox Church in Constantinople and the western Roman Catholic Church in Rome. The split between these two churches still exists today.

Two of the great religions of the world—Judaism and Islam—are iconoclastic and believe that there should be no "graven images" either sculptured or painted. Christianity (circa 700 C.E.) came very close to becoming a religion without any painting and sculpture, but the shadow of the iconoclasts still hangs over the Eastern Orthodox Churches 1,200 years later. Icons (images of holy figures) are the only acceptable forms of art, and then are only to be displayed in front of the church altar. Any three-dimensional art, such as a statue, is still strictly forbidden by the Eastern Orthodox Churches (Boorstin 1992, 189).

- Quick Write: In a short paragraph, describe your favorite statue or work of art. What if someone deliberately destroyed this work of art? What would you think of that person? What do you think should happen to that person? When finished, share your thoughts on this topic with a partner in class and then with the class as a whole.
- Take a Stand: Are you pro-iconoclast or anti-iconoclast? Write a short position paper either attacking or defending iconoclasts.
- Mock Argument: With a partner in class, stage a mock argument between a Christian iconoclast and a Roman patron of the arts (circa 700 C.E.). Outline the major arguments of each side and then present the mock argument to the class.
- What If?: What would happen if Christians had continued to follow the iconoclastic movement—where would art be today? Do a quick write, pair share, and room share on this topic.
- Field Trip: Visit a Roman Catholic and an Eastern Orthodox Christian church today in your community and compare the artwork displayed in each.

- ADV Mock Ecumenical Council: To our thinking today, it is incredible that a simple argument about art could lead to a major 1,200-year split in the Christian Church. In your class, convene a small mock ecumenical council and try to resolve the basic iconoclastic argument between the churches—first with pairs of students, then groups of four, then the whole class.

Note from the Future: Another wave of Christian iconoclastic thinking took place during the sixteenth century during the Protestant Reformation against the Roman Catholic Church (see unit 4).

3.6.5   The Poor Arab Orphan (569–622 C.E.)

How could a poor illiterate Arab orphan rise to be the founder of one of the world's great religions? His hometown of Makkah (Mecca) was a center of idol worshipers, but Mohammad was more influenced by the monotheists around him—both Jewish and Christian. In 610 C.E., he had a vision in which the angel Gabriel proclaimed that he was the prophet of God (Allah). Over the next years, he continued to have visions in which God dictated to him. Close followers then wrote down his visions, which formed the Koran (Qur'an). Many of the Jews and Christians in Makkah became his early followers (Sardar and Malik 1994).

- Quick Write: Have you ever heard of someone having been visited by an angel? In a short paragraph, describe the story you have heard, and then share it with the class.
- Ace Reporter: Imagine you are the ace reporter for the *Medieval Times* newspaper and Mohammad has just come to you with a story of the angel Gabriel appearing to him. Write a newspaper article describing this vision of Mohammad for the next edition of your paper.
- Skeptics: In a team of four students, develop a short skit that illustrates the opposition Mohammad received from some of the people of Mecca (students in the class) who were skeptical of Mohammad's new teachings and of his seeing an angel.
- Letter to the Editor: As one of the early believer of Mohammad's visions, write a letter to editor of the *Medieval Times* describing what happened to Mohammad.
- ADV Research Topic: Do you think that the conditions in Arabia in 622 C.E. made it possible for Mohammad to create a new religion? Or do you think that it was the personal abilities of Mohammad that enabled

him to form this new religion? Use the resources in your library and on the Internet to research and discover what you can find on this topic. When finished, report your findings to the class.

3.6.6   The Koran (Qur'an)

The words of the Koran, said Mohammad, were not his words, but the very words of God. The words of the Koran, according to Mohammad, were not created. They were the words directly from God and therefore the Koran is God. This became the simple central belief of Islam. To become a Moslem is simple—declare belief in the Koran as the word of God and acknowledge that Mohammad is his prophet. It is clear that the Koran was intended to convert the "People of the Book" (Jews and Christians) to Islam: "People of the Book (Jews and Christians)! Our Messenger has come to reveal to you much of what you have hidden of the Book (the Bible), and to forgive you much. A light has come to you from Allah (God) and a Clear Book (the Koran)" (see the Koran, chapter 5:15).

- Quick Write: From your own experience, how easy is it to convert someone from one religion to another religion? Write a short paragraph on your thoughts about this topic and share them with a partner in class. The class as a whole can then come to its own conclusions on how easy it is to change religions.
- People of the Book: In groups of four, study the above passage from the Koran and role-play People of the Book (Jews and Christians) who are reading the Koran for the first time. Create a short skit that illustrates your reaction to this passage and present it to the class. The class as a whole can then speculate if they think that the People of the Book converted to Islam because of this passage.
- ADV Read and Report: Find a copy of the Koran in your library or on the Internet (http://www.mosque.com) and read a section from it. Describe to your class the section of the Koran you read and discuss its meaning.
- ADV Comparison I: Review (see 2.6.6) the concept of Logos—the word is God—of Philo of Alexandria (circa 25 B.C.E.) and compare that with the teachings of Mohammad.
- ADV Comparison II: Using your library and the Internet, compare the Koran to the Bible. What similarities and differences did you find? Be sure to share your findings with your class.

3.6.7   Jewish, Christian, or Muslim?

Believers in Judaism, Christianity, and Islam often do not realize how similar their desert religions are. From the following list, pick out which are from the Jewish Bible (Old Testament), the Christian Bible (New Testament), or the Muslim Bible (the Koran). Mark your answers with a "J," "C," or "K."

1. —— And We said: Oh, Adam! You and your wife dwell in the Garden, and eat freely of its fruits, but do not come near this tree or you will become wrong doers.
2. —— O Children of Israel! Remember that I favored you and preferred you above all creatures.
3. —— And when Moses spent forty nights in solitude, you chose the calf when he had gone from you, and in so doing were wrong doers.
4. —— And when the angels said: O Mary, verily God hath chosen thee and purified thee above all other women.
5. —— The Messiah, Jesus, son of Mary, is only the messenger of God, and his word which he cast upon Mary came from the spirit within him.

(Answer: All of the above five verses are from the Koran.)

- Quick Write: Why are you surprised that all of these verses are from the Koran? Write a short paragraph describing your thoughts on this, and then be prepared to share them with the class.
- Pair Share: With a partner, compare your reactions to each of these verses from the Koran.
- Room Share: Pairs should then share their reactions with the whole class.
- ADV Class Discussion: With Moses, Jesus, and Mary being holy people in the Koran, what does this tell us about the Muslim religion?
- ADV Problem Analysis: With Moses, the holiest man in Judaism, and Jesus, the holiest man in Christianity, both revered in the Koran, why have there been such major battles between Jews, Christians, and Muslims over the past thousand years?

Note: After some reflection, the discussion of this major historical problem can be continued in 3.6.8.

3.6.8   Maimonides (1135–1204 c.e.)

Jews, Christians, and Arabs have always fought each other—correct? Wrong! Maimonides, a Jew from Cordova in Spain, accepted that Jews, Christians, and Muslims all worshiped the same God in different ways and should tolerate one another. Although Jewish, he wrote in Arabic and was the family physician of Saladin, the Muslim leader during the Crusades. He simplified Jewish Law and became the main source of information about medical practices from classical Greece. Maimonides certainly holds the distinction in history of being called a heretic and having his books burned by Jews, Christians, and Muslims all at the same time—because he believed that religions should be practiced with careful reason, not blind faith (Durant 1950, 408–416).

- Quick Write: Why do you think religious leaders from Judaism, Christianity, and Islam would all burn the same man's books? What could he have said that got or made all three religions mad at him?
- Bumper Sticker: Create a bumper sticker that either supports or opposes the ideas of Maimonides.
- Poster Power: Create a poster that illustrates the major ideas of Maimonides and the strong opposition he faced from Jews, Christians, and Muslims alike.
- Press Conference: Go back in time and stage a press conference with Maimonides (a student dressed up in a robe and turban). Leaders from all three religions have just burned his books. Have reporters (students) read about Maimonides (above) and then prepare at least three questions each to ask of him.
- ADV Peace Plan: In teams of four, read more about Maimonides from the library and the Internet, and then develop a peace plan for all three religions—Judaism, Christianity, and Islam—based on the teachings of Maimonides.

3.7.0   CONQUEST AND WARFARE

3.7.1   Attila the Hun

In 450 c.e., Attila and his 300,000 Huns swarmed into western Europe. The Roman Empire was built with large numbers of foot soldiers who fought at close quarters with swords. The Huns were just the opposite.

They fought mounted on fast ponies and fought their battles at a hundred yards with a secret weapon—the powerful composite bow. The combination of large numbers, superior weaponry, and speed on horseback made the Huns of 450–453 C.E. almost invincible—especially to the slow-moving Roman foot soldiers (Mee 1993).

- Quick Write: Take your pick—would you rather be a Hun mounted on a fast pony with a bow and arrow or a heavily armored Roman foot soldier? In a short paragraph, describe the reason for your choice and then share your opinions with the class.
- Poster Power: On a large piece of paper, illustrate the differences between the fighting styles of the Romans and Huns. Label the important major differences.
- Eye Witness: As a Roman living in northern Italy in 451 C.E., write a letter to a friend in Rome describing an attack by the Huns that you recently witnessed.
- Battle Plan: If you were the commander of a Roman army, what preparations would you make for a battle with the Huns?
- Oral Tradition: As an old man and the last remaining Hun who attacked the Roman Empire in 451 C.E., retell for your family and friends (the class) how you attacked the Romans with your friends under the leadership of Attila.
- ADV Historical Comparison: Using resources in your library and on the Internet, make a chart comparing the fighting styles of the Huns of 450 C.E. and the Plains Indians of North America in the 1870s.

3.7.2 Muslim Conquests

By 700 C.E., the armies of Islam conquered virtually all of the Middle East (from Saudi Arabia to Iran) and North Africa (from Egypt to Morocco), an area larger than the Roman Empire. In 711 C.E., a Muslim army under Tariq crossed the Straights of Gibraltar (Arabic: Gibr-al-Tariq = the Rock of Tariq) from Morocco and conquered Spain. The Islamic "conquests" were often quite easy because of the constant battles Christians had with each other over endless religious questions, such as "Was Jesus God or man?" or "Was Mary, the mother of Jesus, holy or not?" Many Christians, as a result, did not offer much resistance to the new Muslim conquerors and willingly followed the much simpler beliefs of Islam. The Muslim armies, however, never had enough power to conquer Europe. A major road-block was in their way for a thousand years—Constantinople (see TLP 3.3.5 and Durant 1950).

- Map Attack: Using an atlas and a blank map of the world, illustrate the swift conquests of the Muslim armies from Mecca and Medina (in modern Saudi Arabia) eastward to Persia (modern Iran) and westward to Morocco and Spain.
- Rumper Sticker: Create a rumper sticker for Tariq's horse as he crossed the Straights of Gibralter (Gibr-al-Tariq) by boat from Morocco to conquer Spain.
- Poster Power: Create a poster advertising Tariq's conquest of Spain in 711 C.E.
- Map Analysis: Using an atlas and a blank map of the world, indicate why the Muslims (in the Middle East) were not able to conquer central and northern Europe. (Clue: Be sure to note the location of Constantinople.)
- ADV What If Analysis?: What would the world be like today, if all of Europe had been conquered by Muslim armies circa 800 C.E.? Would Christianity exist today as a major world religion if this had happened? Use the resources in your library and on the Internet to research this problem and then report your findings to your class

3.7.3   The Crusades (1095–1291 C.E.)

The Crusades were one of the biggest flops in history. The First Crusade was called by Pope Urban II in 1095 C.E. to free Jerusalem from Muslim rule. With the blessings of the Church, the kings of Europe sent armies of young men to recapture the "Holy Land" around Jerusalem. European armies tried four times to conquer the "Holy Land" but failed to hold it very long. The effects of the Crusades, however, were long lasting.

- Quick Write: As a Christian knight riding off to fight in the Crusades, write a letter to your true love describing what it feels like to ride off to battle to fight for a noble cause—the freeing of the Holy Land for Christianity.
- Troubadour: Compose a ballad for the Crusades (and sing it)—in good medieval fashion—how noble it is to go and fight (and die) in

battle with a true love at home waiting for that knight in shining armor who might never return.

- Crusader Spin Doctor: With a partner in class, write and put on a short skit of a knight in shining armor riding off to fight in the Crusades to save the Holy Land for Christians.
- Muslim Counter Spin: With a partner in class, create a short skit that illustrates a Muslim knight with his friends describing the valor of fighting alongside Jewish soldiers against the Christian crusaders to defend the Holy Land in the name of God against foreign invaders.
- Jewish Counter-Counter Spin: As a Jewish fighter with his friends, describe the valor of fighting alongside Muslim soldiers against the Christian crusaders to defend the Holy Land in the name of God against these foreign invaders from Europe.
- Front Page: In a team of four ace reporters from your class, create a front-page edition of the *Medieval Times* newspaper, focusing on the horror of seeing thousands of people either killed or wounded during the Crusades.

3.7.4   The Fourth Crusade—Greed and Glory (1204 c.e.)

By 1204 c.e., the "Christian" crusaders had forgotten that they were on a holy religious quest to capture the Holy Land. They were now fighting for greed and glory, not religion. With the help of the powerful city-state of Venice, the crusaders attacked their richest Christian ally — Constantinople, capital of the Byzantine Empire, robbed it of all its thousand years of accumulated treasures, and carried the treasure back to Western Europe. The illiterate crusaders, however, destroyed a more important treasure: they burned the great libraries of the capital, which contained the last remaining copies of many ancient Greek plays, philosophy, and science (Durant 1950, 602–606).

Historical Comment: Who needs enemies when you have friends like the crusaders?

- Quick Write: Describe how you feel when a close friend turns out to not be a good friend after all.
- Pair Share: Discuss with a partner, for one minute each, which is more important—money, friendship, or personal integrity? What happens when whole nations place money as their most important value? Share your conclusions with the class.

- Diary Entry: As a long-time Christian citizen of Constantinople, express your horror at the barbarian crusaders destroying much of your city. Share your diary entry with the class.
- ADV Historical Research: Using your library and the Internet, research more about the tragic Fourth Crusade and report your findings to class.

3.7.5   The Positive Results of the Crusades

Before the Crusades, most of Western Europe was a vast forest dotted with small feudal kingdoms full of poor, illiterate peasants and serfs, ruled by a small class of nobles. Western Europeans during the Middle Ages did not shave or bathe. The Crusades changed all that. The strange "new" ideas from the East of shaving, bathing, and toilets became popular again—as in ancient Rome. In reality, these old Roman customs had never died out in Byzantine cities such as Constantinople. Other new ideas acquired from the Muslims included gunpowder, the compass, printing, window glass, spices, and citrus fruit. The idea of economic trade suddenly became important. Former feudal serfs who fought in the Crusades now moved to rapidly growing towns and became merchants and craftsmen. The Church grew in wealth from the lands it inherited, but diminished in power as people began take greater interest in money, worldly pleasures, and greater knowledge through reading and writing (Durant 1950, 609–613).

- Quick Song: As a crusader from Western Europe who is the first one in his family to take a bath, compose a song (and sing it to the class) of the great joy of bathing and being squeaky clean.
- Advertising Campaign: In a team of four students who happen to represent the first advertising team during the Middle Ages, develop an advertising campaign to introduce the *new* Persian fruits of apples, oranges, apricots, and grapefruit to Western Europeans. Remember, these new foods were first introduced into Europe by the returning crusaders who acquired them from Muslim merchants. When finished, present your ad campaign to your class.
- Quick Skit: In a group of four students, create a short skit for your thirteenth-century European town (your class) in which the participants are arguing over which was the most important new dis-

covery from the Crusades: gunpowder, paper, window glass, or the compass.

3.7.6 The Tragic Results of the Crusades

The tragic effects of the Crusades are still being felt today around the world.

1. The Crusades lasted for 150 years (1095–1245 C.E.) and caused untold hardship and death to millions of Christians, Jews, and Muslims.
2. The antagonism between the Muslim Middle East and the Christian West today comes largely from the extended fighting and hatred generated during the Crusades.
3. The bigotry, ignorance, and hatred the crusaders showed to the Jewish folk continued down to twentieth-century Nazi Germany and Soviet Russia.
4. The pillaging of Constantinople by the crusaders in 1204 C.E. permanently ended any possibility of reuniting the eastern and western Christian churches.
5. The sack of Constantinople by the crusaders in 1204 C.E. greatly weakened the thousand-year-old Byzantine Empire and opened it to a final conquest by the Muslims. It no longer provided the strong Eastern shield of protection for Europe from Muslim conquests. Only a new Mongol threat from the East enabled Constantinople and Europe to be safe from Muslim attacks for several hundred years more (see TLP 3.7.10).

- Rumper Sticker: Create a rumper sticker for horses during the Middle Ages reminding crusaders not to pillage, steal, and rape.
- Poet's Corner: Compose a sad poem about loved ones lost during the Crusades.
- Newspaper Reporter: As a reporter for the *Medieval Times* newspaper, interview Jews, Christians, and Muslims (students) who experienced the mass destruction of the Crusades and write an editorial regarding the Crusades for your newspaper.
- ADV Pro and Con: Conduct a class symposium on the pros and cons of the Crusades. Were they more beneficial than harmful or were they more harmful than beneficial? Teams of four students

should conduct their own research in the library and on the Internet, come to their own conclusions, and then present their findings to the whole class.

3.7.7   Genghis Khan (circa 1160–1227 C. E.)

The recent twentieth century was certainly a bloody century—but so was the thirteenth century. The crusaders killed as many people as they could in the Middle East, but they were quickly followed by the Mongols of Genghis Khan. As the close relatives of the Huns, the Mongols used good leadership, superior organization, fast ponies, and excellent skills in archery to quickly conquer China and central Asia in a few short years. The Mongols had all of Asia and the Middle East frightened. Beijing, the capital of China, was founded by the Mongols. The Great Wall of China was constructed to prevent further Mongol invasions. Hulagu, grandson of Genghis Khan, sacked Baghdad for a week (1258 C.E.) and ended the great cultural flowering and military strength of the Muslims for several hundred years (see Edwards 1996, 5–37).

Historical Note from the Future: Europe's eastern shield, Constantinople, was no more than a shell after the crusaders attacked it in 1204. Constantinople, and possibly Europe, could have easily fallen to Muslim conquest, but the Byzantines and Europeans were lucky. The Mongols began to attack the Middle East in 1218 C.E. and even captured the capital of Islam—Baghdad—in 1258 C.E. After the Mongol attacks, it took two hundred years for the Muslims to recover their strength and finally capture Constantinople in 1453.

- Quick Write: As a Muslim standing on the city wall of Baghdad in 1258, describe your terror as you see the massive Mongol armies approach your city.
- Rumper Sticker: Create a rumper sticker for the backside of Hulagu Khan's horse.
- Graffiti: On a piece of paper, create a wall graffiti that urges Muslim warriors to fight their best against the armies of Hulagu Khan.
- Mongol Marksmen and Markswomen: Mongol men and women were excellent marksmen firing arrows from bows and traveling at full speed on ponies. With the archery equipment at your school, have your whole class practice shooting arrows at a fixed target.

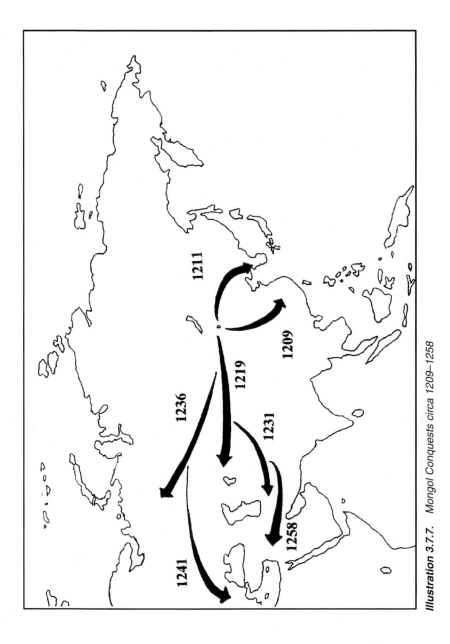

Illustration 3.7.7. Mongol Conquests circa 1209–1258

- Role Play: As a male or female Mongol warrior, describe what it feels like to ride full speed on a pony and shoot an arrow at a target behind you. Imagine ten thousand mounted Mongols attacking all at the same time.
- You Were There: As the television anchorperson for the hit show "You Were There," interview several witnesses (students) to the Mongol capture of Baghdad in 1258 C.E.:
  1. Fatima—the rich first wife (one of twenty) of the sultan of Baghdad
  2. Ali—a Muslim solider who saw the main Mongol attack and escaped alive
  3. Suliman—a Muslim merchant who saw Baghdad being burned to the ground
  4. Ibn Sina—a scholar who saw the great scientific, medical, and mathematical writings of Islam going up in flames
  5. Tamarin—A strong female Mongol warrior who participated in the attack on Baghdad
- ADV Mongol Map Attack: Using your library and a historical atlas, use a blank map of Asia and the Middle East to trace the routes of the Mongol attacks on the rest of the world (see Edwards 1996, 6). Measure in miles or kilometers the great distances covered by the Mongol armies and compare these distances with distances between major cities in the United States.

3.8.0   TRAGEDY AND DISASTER

3.8.1   A Jewish Holocaust of 1095–1096 C.E.

On the way to the Crusades, Christian armies from Europe often killed Jews they found in towns along the way. Why? They did so, they said, because the Jews killed Jesus. In reaction to this holocaust, Jewish soldiers joined with the Muslims to fight against the Christian invaders of the Holy Land during the Crusades.

Historical Correction: The Romans, not the Jews, killed Jesus (see Mark 15:16–20 and Jospehus 1988, 264), the major historical source of the era, states specifically: "Pilot condemned him (Jesus) to be crucified and to die." The ancient Jewish death penalty for religious reasons was stoning to death. The ancient Roman death penalty for rebels against Roman rule was crucifixion. Few, if any, of the crusaders of

1096 knew how to read or write—only priests were allowed to do this. If the crusaders knew how to read, they could have read the Bible themselves to verify who killed Jesus. They, however, did not do so and let their prejudice overrule their reason.

- Poster: Make a poster and a slogan illustrating why is it dangerous to believe a rumor without checking whether it is accurate or not. Example: "Don't Act! Check your facts!"
- Diary Entry: As a Jewish teenager in medieval France, describe the terror of seeing your friends and family being killed by the Christian crusaders. When finished, share your diary entry with your class.
- Pair Share: With a partner from your class, discuss for one minute each why it is dangerous for people (like the crusaders) to *not* know how to read and write.
- Fighting Prejudice: In a team of four students, devise a plan to help students at your school stop negative rumors about other students. Share your ideas with the class and the whole student body.

A Sad Historical Irony: During the Crusades of 1095–1204 C.E., Muslims and Jews fought on the same side to defend the Holy Land (Israel/Palestine) against the Christians. During the twentieth century, Jewish forces—with American Christian support—fought Muslim forces for the control of the same land.

3.8.2   Black Death (Bubonic Plague) of 1331–1369 C.E.

The Black Death (bubonic plague) of the late Middle Ages killed about twenty-five million people. It first broke out in China in 1331 and killed half of its population. Venice, after the Crusades, controlled the trade between Europe and Asia. The plague hit Venice first and spread northward during 1348 to 1349. Subsequent outbreaks occurred in 1361–1362 and 1369. Milan (in Italy) was spared. Bristol in England was nearly wiped out. Nearly one-third of Europe's population perished. The plague quickly ended feudalism in many places—there was no one left to till the fields for the nobles. Anybody who survived the plague fled to the growing cities of Europe, such as Venice, Florence, London, and Paris (McNeil 1977).

The only people who seem to have survived the bubonic plague of the late Middle Ages in any substantial numbers were the Jews, because of their house-cleaning rituals of *purem* before Passover, which discouraged plague-infected rats from entering their homes just before the outbreak of the plague each spring.

- Quick Write: Imagine if one-third of the people around you suddenly died of an unknown cause. How would you feel? What would you do?
- Medieval Artist: As the major artist in your town during the Middle Ages, record for history the horrid scene of so many people dying of the plague.
- Playwrights: With four other students, write and present a short skit to your class that depicts the bubonic plague infecting a town.
- Medieval Rumor Mill: Fear creates rumors and rumors create more fear. The teacher can start a rumor in class by whispering the name of a popular student to one student and then have the rumor spread across the room—that person in class caused the bubonic plague. A class discussion should follow the spread of the rumor using the following questions:
  1. Is the rumor true? (Of course it is not!)
  2. Why do people believe rumors or want to believe rumors?
  3. Why are ethnic minorities and old people often the target for such rumors?
  4. What can be done to stop such rumors?
- What If?: In teams of two, imagine that you are medical doctors from the Middle Ages. What would you start looking for as the cause of the Black Death? What would you do to aid people who suddenly fall ill with the bubonic plague? What would you begin to do to prevent further spread of the plague? Share your ideas with the other medical doctors (students) in the room.
- ADV Epidemiologist: Research the background of the causes and cures of the bubonic plague of the mid-fourteenth century. Compare this epidemic with other large world epidemics, such as the Spanish Influenza of 1918. Report your findings to the class.

3.9.0   EXPLORATION AND DISCOVERY

3.9.1   Marco Polo (1254–1323?)—Myth or Reality?

A story from a prison in Genoa (Italy) in 1298 fired the imagination of Europeans in the late Middle Ages. It was written in French by a prisoner named Rustichello. A fellow prisoner by the name of Marco Polo had told him the tale of his travels to China, where he had lived some seventeen years in the service of Kublai Khan, the Mongol emperor of China. Rustichello knew how to embellish a story and make it exciting; as a result, *The Travels of Marco Polo* became a best-seller of the Middle Ages. It was laboriously hand copied into almost every major language of the time (Boorstin 1983, 134–138). Some recent scholars believe that Rustichello, and perhaps Marco himself, made up all or large parts of the story (see Wood 1996). Whether true or not, Marco Polo's story had a tremendous influence on the history of the world. Kings and adventurers across Europe had the story read to them and burned with desire to explore new lands.

Historical Note from the Future: Virtually every explorer of the fifteenth century read the book or had it told to him. In 1477, *The Travels of Marco Polo* became one of the first books, after the Bible, to be printed. Today, after seven hundred years, the book still remains very popular—even if it is a fake.

- Adventure Write: Think of the most exotic place you would like to visit in your lifetime. Write down the name of this place and why you would like to travel there. (People during the late Middle Ages considered Marco Polo's trip to be the most exotic adventure possible.)
- Map Attack: On a blank map of Asia, trace the route of the Silk Road traveled by Marco Polo and his brothers from Constantinople through Samarkand (Uzbekistan) to the Mongol capital of Karakoram.
- Pair Share: With a partner, describe the most important book you ever read and then share your discussion with the class.
- ADV Research: How can a simple, possibly fictional, book have stimulated humans to begin exploring the world and think about their planet in a whole new way? Conduct interviews with people you know and research this topic in your library and on the Internet. When finished, present your findings to the class.

3.9.2 Ibn Batutta (1304–1369)

Why is so much written about Marco Polo, when a contemporary of his from Tangier (Morocco) traveled over 75,000 miles across the globe in twenty-nine years—over three times the distance traveled by Marco Polo? Ibn Batutta traveled to Mecca in 1325, became a Muslim judge, worked his way to India, then China, then back to Mecca, and back to Morocco, where he traveled north to Muslim Spain and then south across the Sahara Desert to Timbuktu and returned to Fez, Morocco, where he retired to write an account of his travels in 1354. No one questions whether Ibn Batutta's travels are real—the original manuscript of his travels, written in Arabic, still exists today in the Bibliotheque Nationale in Paris, France (Abercrombie 1991, 2–49).

- Travel Wish List: Make a list of ten places in the world you would like to visit and then show how you could visit each place in one long trip on a blank map of the world.
- When finished, measure the mileage you plan to travel to see if it is greater than the 75,000 miles traveled by Ibn Batutta during the fourteenth century.
- Map Attack: On a blank map of the world, trace the major routes of Ibn Batutta's fourteenth-century journeys from the above description. Start with his home in Tangier, Morocco, and end it 75,000 miles later at Fez, Morocco. Be sure to label the major places he visited.
- ADV Research: If Ibn Batutta traveled three times as far as Marco Polo, and there is no question that he really did travel to all these places, why did Marco Polo become famous, and only a few historians know about Ibn Batutta? Research your library and the Internet to try to find the answer to this problem. When finished, present your findings to your class. (Hint: Could it be an ethnic bias, such as that Marco Polo was a European Christian and Ibn Batutta was a Muslim from Morocco, North Africa?)

3.10.0   INVENTION AND REVOLUTION

3.10.1   The Power of Zero

The numbers one through nine first appeared in India 2,000 years ago, but without any place value and without the concept of zero. Sometime around 400 C.E., Indian scholars began to use a dot or zero as a placeholder to indicate nothing. For the first time in history, it was easy to add, subtract, multiply, and divide by 10, 100, or 1,000. In 773 C.E., an ambassador from India brought the gift of numbers and calculation to the Muslim Caliph Mansur in Baghdad. Arab scholars in Caliph Mansur's court immediately recognized the importance of this gift and studied it

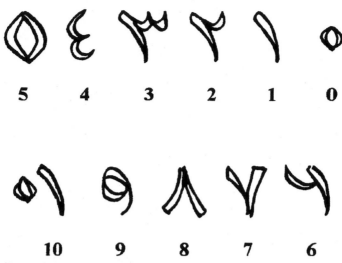

Illustration 3.10.1.   Arabic Numbers (read from right to left)

intensely. Within a few short years, an Arab scholar named Al-Khwarizmi (circa 780–850) wrote the first major book about mathematics, *The Book of Addition and Subtraction by Indian Methods*. The book was translated into Latin in Muslim Spain and quickly spread to Europe. Al-Khwarizmi, as a result, became recognized as the father of modern mathematics. The modern mathematical word "algorism" is based on Algorismus, Al-Khwarizmi's Latin name (Guedj 1996, 45–54).

- Roman Math: Add together XIII plus CIX (Answer: CXXII). Is that tough to do? Now try 13 + 109 (Answer: 122). Why is this Indian/Arab method so much easier? (It's the use of place values 10 and 100, along with the concept of zero, that makes it easy.)
- Arab Numbers: Write the numbers from zero to ten in Arabic numbers. For a hint, see illustration 3.10.1—and remember that zero in Arabic numbers is a dot and that Arabic is read from right to left.
- T Chart Comparison: What differences do you see between Arabic numbers and the numbers we use today? Using a T chart, write modern numbers from zero to ten down the left-hand side of the T chart and the parallel Arabic numbers down the right side. Looking very carefully at the Arabic equivalent of each, describe how each Arabic number is different from our modern numbers.

- Arabic Mathematician: Now that you are a scholar in Arabic numbers, write the current year using Arabic numbers and then write down the year you were born in Arabic numbers. (Remember that Arabic is written from right to left.) When finished, share your work with the class.

3.10.2   Islamic Medicine

Good Christians during the Middle Ages never washed. Cleanliness was sinful. A person was sick because of the evil deeds committed by that person. These were major Christian beliefs during the Middle Ages in Europe. Little wonder the age was considered the "Dark Ages." Muslim physicians in the Middle East, on the other hand, conducted major studies of ancient Greek medicine and made great progress in improving Greek medical practices. Muslim and excommunicated Nestorian Christian doctors at Jundisharpur—the major medical school of the Middle Ages—made major medical improvements. Al-Rashid (786–809) and his son Al-Ma'Mon established a translating bureau to translate Greek works into Arabic. By the end of the ninth century, all of the major Greek medical works were translated into Arabic. Some of the more notable achievements were as follows (Tschanz 1997):

1. Al-Rashid established the first modern hospital circa 805 C.E.
2. Al-Razi (841–926 C.E.) wrote more than 100 medical books, including *The Diseases of Children* and a twenty-five-volume encyclopedia of medicine.
3. Ibn Sina (980–1037) (Avicenna in Latin) wrote the million-word *Canon of Medicine,* which codified all existing medical knowledge from Greece, Syria, Persia, and India.

Note from the Future: The medical works of Al-Rashid, Al-Razi, and Ibn Sina became the medical bibles for the Middle East and Europe for 400 years.

- Quick Write: Imagine, for a moment, what life would be like without modern medicine. In a short paragraph, describe what you think it would be like if superstition was used instead of modern medicine.
- Poster Power: Create a poster that illustrates the power of modern medicine, introduced into Europe at the end of the Middle Ages by the major Arab medical doctors.

- Music Mart: Compose a medieval ballad praising the work of the early Arab medical doctors for bringing modern medicine to the rest of the world.
- You Were There: As the host of this top TV show of the Middle Ages, your guests for today's show are three of the great Muslim medical doctors from Baghdad: Al-Rashid, Al-Razi, and Ibn Sina (students dressed up as Muslim scholars). Be sure the members of your studio audience (students in class) have three questions each for these honored guests from the Middle Ages.
- ADV Historical Research: Using resources in your library and on the Internet, discover what else you can find out about early Arabic medicine and scientific research, during a time when little or none of it was being conducted in Europe.

3.10.3   Jewish Translations of Arabic to Latin (1000–1200 C.E.)

The flowering of the Renaissance in Europe during the fifteenth century might not have happened if it were not for the intellectual enlightenment and religious toleration between Jews, Christians, and Muslims practiced by two very small Christian kingdoms during the Middle Ages. In an era known for its ignorance and religious bigotry, the kingdoms of Toledo in Spain under Alfonso X and the kingdoms of the Two Sicilies under King Roger II in Salerno provided the crucial intellectual background and tolerant climate needed to stimulate Europe's long, slow road out of the Middle Ages.

In Toledo, King Alfonso X had the great wisdom to sponsor a school to translate major Greek and Arabic scientific, mathematical, and medical books from Arabic to the dominant language of Europe—Latin. The translation work in Toledo from Arabic to Latin was done primarily by Jewish scholars and Gerard of Cremona (1140–1187), who were fluent in both Arabic and Latin. Some of the major works translated at Toledo were *Commentaries on Aristotle* by Ibn Rushd (Averroes), works on algebra and mathematics by Al-Khwarizmi (from whose name we get the mathematical term *algorithm*), and *The Canon* of Ibn Sina (Avicenna), which became Europe's medical standard for 500 years. These works by the school in Toledo under the tolerant Christian ruler Alfonso X were to become the backbone of the intellectual growth of the Renaissance in Europe.

In Salerno, in the Cloister of Monte Casino, under the tolerant and enlightened Christian King Roger II, major translation work from Arabic to Latin was also done by such scholars as Leo Africanus (1020–1087). In both kingdoms, Arabs, Christians, and Jews were openly accepted and worked closely together to translate the crucial new medical and scientific information from the Middle East that would eventually awaken Europe from its long intellectual slumber (Abercrombie 1988).

- Map Attack: Use an atlas to locate Toledo, Spain, and Salerno, Italy, on a map of Europe. On a blank map of Europe, put large stars next to these cities because of the important work these towns did advancing science and encouraging tolerance in Europe.
- Quick Write: Using your knowledge of the locations of the translation schools in Toledo and Salerno, describe in a short paragraph the importance of the location of these two towns between the Muslim world in southern Spain and North Africa and the European Christian world to the north.
- Bumper Sticker: Create a bumper sticker cheering on the work being done in Toledo and Salerno during the Middle Ages.
- Poster Power: Create a poster that illustrates the importance to history of the translation work done at Toledo and Salerno during the Middle Ages.
- What If?: With a partner in class, discuss for one minute each what would have happened to European history if the translating schools in Toledo and Salerno never existed. When finished, share your ideas with your whole class for their consideration.
- ADV Translator: With the help of a student in your classroom who knows a language other than English, work to translate a short poem from that language into English. Describe in a quick write how difficult the task of translation from one language to the next can be.
- ADV Historical Research: Using resources from your library and the Internet, research the question why Christian Europe had so much to learn from the Muslim Middle East in terms of science and medicine. Why did Christians in Europe at the same time develop so much hatred against the Muslims that they attacked them repeatedly during the Crusades after 1095 C.E.? When finished, report your findings to your class.
- ADV Interpretative Research: Why are the translating schools of Toledo and Salerno rarely mentioned in many textbooks of European history? Search your school library and the Internet to see if you can

find any information on this question. When finished, share your findings with your class for their general discussion.

3.10.4   St. Thomas Aquinas (1225–1274 C.E.)

One of the most powerful thinkers to emerge during the thousand years of the Middle Ages was Thomas Aquinas. Benefiting from the Arabic to Latin translations done at Toledo and Salerno, he pulled all of the great Jewish and Muslim thinking of his age from writers such as Maimonides and Avicenna together and concluded that the ancient Greeks, such as Aristotle, were correct. Humans must use their brains to understand the world around them. Weaker men would have been burnt at the stake by the Church, but Aquinas survived. Aquinas applied the classical Greek thinking of Aristotle to Christianity and accepted rationalism along with faith. This was the beginning of modern science. With Aquinas, Europe began to move out of the Middle Ages and into the Renaissance.

Note from the Future: As a result of his stand on reason, Thomas Aquinas is considered to be a father of the Renaissance, which was still 100 years into the future. The Church also began to change and sainted him in 1323; however, it was nearly 600 years later when they finally declared his teachings to be part of Church philosophy in 1921 (Durant 1950, 961–978).

- Quick Write: Describe an example from your life when you wish you had used your brain rather than your emotions. Why is it better to stop and think for a moment rather than use pure emotion?
- Pair Share: Share your regret not to use reason with a partner and then with the class as a whole.
- Bumper Sticker: Create a medieval bumper sticker for ox carts supporting Aquinas.
- Art Mart: Create a drawing or painting that illustrates Aquinas's contribution to world history.
- Quick Skit: With a team of four students from your class, develop and present a short dramatization that illustrates Aquinas's trust in reason and the reluctance of the Church to accept anything other than religious faith.
- ADV Research Report: Using your library and the Internet as resources, research in more detail the influence Aquinas had on the Middle Ages. When finished, report your findings to the class.

3.11.0 ART AND CREATIVE THOUGHT

3.11.1 Hagia Sophia (537 C.E.)

The masterpiece of the early Middle Ages was the Hagia Sophia church, dedicated by Justinian and Theodora in 537 C.E. It was built by Justinian and Theodora following the Nika revolt and burning of Constantinople in 532 C.E.—an example of catastrophe inviting innovation. Key to the architectural design of the Hagia Sophia was how to balance a dome over a square structure; this became the great contribution of Byzantine architecture. The major problem with the Hagia Sophia was that the Byzantines had forgotten how to cast in cement—the technique that had enabled Rome to build such magnificent domed strictures only 300 years before. As a result, the Hagia Sophia was constructed out of stone, brick, iron, and lead—magnificently well done, but not anything like the grand elegance of the Pantheon of Hadrian 400 years before.

Historical Irony from the Future: Ironically, in 726 C.E., the great mosaic images of the Hagia Sophia were plastered over for a time until the fury of the iconoclasts passed—this aided in their preservation. The Muslim Turks aided its preservation in 1453 C.E. by again plastering over the great mosaics and turning the great structure into a *masjid* (mosque). The enlightened Turkish government turned the Hagia Sophia into a museum in 1935 and now we all can see the great Byzantine mosaics of 537 C.E. in Istanbul in all their splendor.

- IQ Test: In a short paragraph, describe how you put a round object on square walls? (This was the basic problem of designing the Hagia Sophia church in Constantinople.)
- Modeling: Make a model or diorama of the Hagia Sophia church out of cardboard.
- Mosaics: Gather many pieces of colored paper from old magazines and cut them into small half-inch squares. With a glue stick, make a picture of a friend or someone you admire using these small squares of colored paper, using the technique of Byzantine mosaics.
- Field Work: Find the oldest building in your town. How old is it? Is it being maintained for history? Imagine what it will look like in 1,500 years.
- ADV Historical Research: Using the resources in your library and on the Internet, examine in more detail the contributions of Byzantine in the fields of art and architecture.

3.11.2   The Medieval Troubadours

Although frowned on by the Church, music continued to flourish outside of the Church. A major musical medium outside of the Church was the troubadour. Singers and musicians from the poorest peasant to the most noble of princes performed songs of the troubadours during the Middle Ages. Over 2,500 such songs and poems still exist. Such troubadour songs and verses were extremely popular in that they were sung in local languages, such as early French and early German. In many cases, these early troubadour songs and verses represent the first written evidence of languages such as French and German. The troubadours sang of princely valor and true love of fair maidens—and everybody listened (maybe even the priests did so secretly behind closed doors).

Classroom Note: For troubadour classroom background music, the four-CD set entitled *The Medieval Experience* (Archiv Production 449 082 2 by Deutsche Grammophon) is a good source.

- Song Writer: Write a song for someone you love secretly in the style of the troubadours.
- Costumer: Create a troubadour costume.
- Musician: With a mandolin or guitar, pretend you are a troubadour singing the songs of what you have seen and heard during the Middle Ages.
- T Chart: Compare the troubadours of the Middle Ages to the musical groups of today. Use a T chart to compare how they are similar and different.
- ADV Historical Research: Using your library and the Internet, research how the Catholic Church's opposition to joyful music and troubadours who composed thousands of joyful songs throughout the Middle Ages could exist side by side. When finished, report your findings to the class.

3.11.3   The Holy Calligraphy and Tessellations of Islam

The Koran makes no mention of images, but Muslims from the "Traditions of the Prophet" (*hadiths*) became strong iconoclastic believers. The *word* rather than the *image* of God became the center of Islam. Written Arabic was developed in order to express the words of the Koran. As a result, written Arabic, itself, became the major art form of

Illustration 3.11.3a. Arabic Calligraphy, circa 1300. Translated [right to left]: Wala ghaleb illa Allah, "No one is a winner, but God" The Alhambra Palace, Granada, Spain

Muslims (calligraphy), along with repeating patterns of nonrepresentational designs—tessellations.

- Personal Calligraphy: Make a beautiful design out of your name and share it with your class.
- Arabic Calligraphy: In Arabic, the beautiful saying in the illustration says: "No one is a winner, but God!"
- Practice Calligraphy: Practice Arabic calligraphy yourself by repeating the example of Arabic art across a page—remember that Arabic is written from right to left.
  Historical Note: The inscription here is taken from the magnificent Alhambra Palace in Granada, Spain (circa 1300 C.E.), where it is repeated over and over again on the palace walls.
- Personal Tessellation: Write the initials of your name into a beautiful triangle or circular design. Now repeat this design upside-down and right-side-up to fill up a page.
- Arabic Tessellation: Make a beautiful design on a page—it cannot be of a flower or any living thing—and then repeat this design upside-down and right-side-up to fill up the page.
- Recreation of a Muslim Palace: Display the calligraphy and tessellations developed by your class on the walls of your room as an example of what a Muslim palace during the Middle Ages might have looked like.

Illustration 3.11.3b. *African Arabian Tessellations from the Alhambra in Granada, Spain, circa 1200*

- ADV Photo Research: Go to the library to search for photographs of the Alhambra Palace in Granada, Spain (constructed 1248–1354), one of the most beautiful palaces in the world and the finest expression of Islamic calligraphy and tessellations. Share what you find with your class. (See Abercrombie 1988 for a good source of pictures and a history of the Alhambra.)
- ADV Comparative Research: Compare the artwork of the Middle Ages in Europe—gothic churches, stained-glass windows, and statues of Jesus—with the art of the Muslim world during the Middle Ages—calligraphy and tessellations.

3.11.4   The Gothic Cathedral

All the early Christian churches of the Middle Ages were built with heavy walls and small windows, and were dark inside. Suger (1081?–1151), the abbot of St. Denis near Paris, France, was no architect, but he disliked these early dark, heavy Romanesque churches; he wanted to build a church that showed the light of God. His new church would have tall, slender, pointed arches and spires that pointed to God.

The western major entrance to the church would have three large arched doors topped by a large rose window of stained glass. Because the massive walls of the early churches were too heavy to have large windows, Suger's new church would have flying buttresses to support thin, tall walls separated by large stained-glass windows. Each stained-glass window would tell a major story of Christianity. Suger's new church revolutionized church architecture and was copied in new forms all across Europe—and represents some of the most magnificent buildings in the world today ever created by humans.

- Art Mart: Based on an illustration of a Gothic cathedral, make a drawing of a Gothic cathedral to display on your classroom wall.
- Field Work: Find out if there is a church in your area that is patterned after one of the great Gothic cathedrals of Europe and visit it.
- Model Making: Make a model out of cardboard of a tall Gothic cathedral with flying buttresses.
- Stained-Glass Windows: With colored pieces of paper, make a model of a stained-glass window that tells a story of some one you admire.
- Stained-Glass Demo: Find out if someone in the art department of your school knows how to make stained glass and demonstrate the process to the class.
- Imagine: Imagine you are visiting Salisbury Cathedral in England, one of the greatest Gothic cathedrals. In a poem, describe your feelings as you enter this great cathedral constructed more than 800 years ago.
- ADV Comparative Research #1: Classic Greek temples always look very similar to each other, and yet Greece had no centralized state. Gothic cathedrals, on the other hand, always looked much different from each other, even those constructed in the same state. Use your library and the Internet to see what you can find on this historical problem, and then report your findings to your class.
- ADV Comparative Research #2: Which do you think are greater— Greek temples, Roman temples, Gothic cathedrals, or traditional Japanese temples? Defend your reasons. Why do you think they are so different from each other?

3.11.5 The *Divine Comedy*

Dante Alighieri's (1265–1321) masterpiece, *Divine Comedy,* is a transition point between the Middle Ages and the Renaissance. Really, it is a long triple-rhyming poem—the first written in a European language

(Italian) that focuses on the dominant religious ideas of Europe during the Middle Ages. While guided through seven layers of heaven and seven layers of hell, Dante, in his masterpiece, realizes that humans freely decide the direction of their lives, which ultimately sends them toward heaven or hell. The Christian God of the Middle Ages still dominates the *Divine Comedy*, but human reason, from the Renaissance, gives humans the choice of deciding the direction of their fate. Dante is truly the bridge between the Middle Ages and the Renaissance (Boorstin 1992, 255–264).

Note from the Future: Dante's *Divine Comedy* is to this day considered to be a masterpiece of Italian poetry—800 years later. Dante's story of human choices does not fade and remains a great book to read in our own day.

- Quick Write: In a short paragraph, quickly describe what you would like more than anything in the world and the worst possible thing that could happen to you—your personal heaven and your personal hell.
- Poster Power: Illustrate in a poster why Dante represents a major transition between the Middle Ages and the Renaissance.
- You Were There: As a roving reporter for Timeless TV Network, conduct an interview with Dante (a fellow student) and present it to your class.
- ADV Reading Research: Check out a copy of Dante's *Divine Comedy* from your library and identify which parts of it reflect the Middle Ages and which reflect the Renaissance.

3.12.0   SUCCESSES AND FAILURES OF THE MIDDLE AGES

3.12.1   Success or Failure?

- This is the competitive quiz show that challenges teams to list as many reasons as possible why a person, place, or thing is the most important success or greatest failure of the Middle Ages.
  1. Each student team of four draws the name of a medieval person, place, or thing from a hat.
  2. Each team calls out its name and the scorekeeper puts it on the board as the team's name.
  3. Using any books or materials available, each student team has fifteen minutes to make as long a list as possible of reasons why the name is the most important of the medieval era.

4. The medieval names to be used can be as follows or developed from a larger list:

Justinian	Hagia Sophia	iconoclasts
Arab mathematics	Arab science	St. Augustine
the Crusades	the Black Death	St. Thomas Aquinas
gunpowder	the compass	the hourglass
Attila	Dante	Maimonides
Charlemagne	Ibn Batutta	Genghis Khan

Fall of Constantinople (29 May 1453)
Translating schools at Toledo and Salerno
Europe's loss of Greek writing and thinking

5. A scorekeeper will keep track how many answers each team gives on the board.

6. The team with the most number of "valid" supporting reasons wins a free trip to the library.

3.13.0   MAJOR WORLD PROBLEMS FOR THE MIDDLE AGES

3.13.1   The Problem of Intolerance

Religious intolerance during the Middle Ages was brutal, inhumane, and long lasting. At first, Christian iconoclasts destroyed only classical works of art and paintings. As the Church became more powerful, however, the intolerance turned toward other Christians with even the smallest differences of religious opinion. As the Christian clergy were forbidden to shed blood, "burning at the stake" became the means of punishing other Christians (heretics) who shared different beliefs. In 1095 C.E., the Church turned to attacking the Muslims controlling the Holy Land (today's Israel/Palestine) with even bloodier results.

Note from the Future: Today, religious intolerance by all three monotheistic religions (Judaism, Christianity, and Islam) seems to be inescapable. Each believes that it has the one true God and will not accept the beliefs of other religions.

• An Inquisition (simulated):
  1. The Inquisition has just met and concluded that all students wearing red in your class are to stand in a far corner of the room.

2. The Inquisition (the rest of the class) must decide what punishment (simulated) the "Red Wearers" should receive for wearing the forbidden color.
3. All "Red Wearers" must then stand in front of the class to receive their punishment (simulated).
4. There is no defense for the "Red Wearers." The Inquisition has found them guilty and they must receive their punishment (simulated).
5. The Inquisition (simulated) is now over. All students may take their original seats.

- The Inquisition Debriefed:
  1. Quick Write: Both the members of the Inquisition and the "Red Wearers" should write down their impressions of their role in the simulation.
  2. Pair Share: Each two students should share their impressions of the simulation with each other and then with the class as a whole.
  3. Class Debrief: What was wrong with the Inquisition? What human rights did not exist with the Inquisition? What if the "Blue Wearers" were the next to be punished? How can we identify inquisitions before they start? How can an inquisition be stopped once it gets started?

Note from the Future: The Inquisition during the Middle Ages was a religious one. Throughout history, inquisitions tend to appear when certain people become intolerant of other people's beliefs. Sadly, we will see more inquisitions in the future whenever a few people believe in an ideology more than they believe in human rights.

3.13.2 The Problem of Poverty

The poor did not have a chance during the Middle Ages. Society was strictly divided between the nobility (usually rich) and the peasants (almost always poor), with no chance of moving up the social ladder. The Church (rich) also preached to the commoners (poor) that it was good to be poor. How could the poor improve themselves? They couldn't! The Church considered education—reading and writing—to be sinful for everyone except the priests. Even earning money by charging interest (usury) was forbidden. The poor peasants were really stuck during the Middle Ages.

- Quick Write: Write down five ways that poor people in the United States today can pull themselves out of poverty.
- Pair Share: Share your quick write with a neighbor in the class and then with the whole class.
- Newspaper Editorial: As the ace reporter for the *Medieval Times* newspaper, visit a poor peasant family (students in class) during the Middle Ages and report on their living conditions and what plans they have for the future.
- Group Project: In groups of four (poor peasants), make a plan to escape from poverty during the Middle Ages and present your plan to the Peasant Assembly (the class). The group with the best plan gets to escape from poverty and join the Crusades.

3.14.0   MEDIEVAL ANTECEDENTS FOR THE FUTURE

3.14.1   The Economic Revolution of the Middle Ages

During the Middle Ages, Europe was transformed from vast forests and feudal estates into thriving economic towns where individual entrepreneurs began to thrive. Great fairs of cobblers, dressmakers, and tailors began on a small scale the free-enterprise capitalism that would come to dominate our own century.

- Role Play: Transform your classroom into a medieval faire with each student presenting a skill (dressmaking, candle making), a talent (musician, artist, jester), or merchandise (candy, popcorn) to sell for money in a small, early example of capitalism.
- ADV Comparative Essay: Compare the early capitalism of the medieval faire with the capitalism of the late twentieth and early twenty-first centuries.

3.14.2   Results of the Inquisition

It is sad to report that the brutal Inquisitions in France, Spain, and Italy were successful. Beliefs about God other than those approved by the Roman Catholic Church were burned out (at the stake) and these countries remain overwhelmingly Catholic today. The Inquisition, however, was not as strong in the Germanic states to the north and different ideas of a Christian God were not eliminated.

Note from the Future: Three hundred years later, in these same Germanic states, the Protestant Reformation successfully rose up and became independent from the main church in Rome.

- You Were There: As the anchorperson on the prime TV news program of the Middle Ages, Torquemada, the head of the Inquisition in Spain (a student in disguise) has granted you and your studio audience an interview. Each member of the studio audience should have three questions ready to ask His Excellency about the role of the Inquisition in the Catholic Church. Each of the members of the audience must be careful, however; if you rub him the wrong way, he might test your stamina on the rack.
- ADV The Futurist: Research your library and the Internet on information concerning the Catholic Church's current view of the Inquisition. Report your findings to the class.

3.14.3   Endpoint of the Middle Ages/Start of the Renaissance

The following are advanced research questions to answer about the end of the Middle Ages and the beginning of the Renaissance.

- ADV Pick a year for the end of the Middle Ages and the beginning of the Renaissance and defend why you think that is the changeover date. (Reality Note: Even historians cannot agree on a date for this change.)
- ADV Why is Dante considered the transition point between the Middle Ages and the Renaissance?
- ADV What would have happened if the Church had burned Thomas Aquinas for heresy rather than making him a saint? Since he is considered the father of the Renaissance, would the Renaissance have taken place without his leadership? Use library and Internet resources to research this question and report your findings to the class.

3.14.4   Is Humankind Ready to Advance?

It is now time to judge whether or not humankind is ready to advance into the next era.

- Five members from around Middleville (the class) will state their basic viewpoints of whether or not enough advances have been made during the Middle Ages to move forward. The five illustrious members are as follows:

1. Letoc Betrink, the archconservative of Middleville, believes that humankind has gone far enough with enough progress. Betrink believes strongly that the good old days were the best and that humankind needs to hold strongly to past values and beliefs.

2. Motar Derudzuk, one of the rising young voices in the town, is a more moderate conservative who believes that we need to be very cautious with any change and be very sure that no harm will come to Middleville if change takes place. Motar is willing to accept some change, but only in very small amounts and only when the time is right—and wants to be the one to decide when that time will come.

3. Pewik Wookbot, the wishy-washy middle-of-the-roader around town, is willing to accept change for a few minutes after one speaker, but may have a change of mind in an instant to oppose change after another speaker has finished.

4. Yatdark Vatsmeer, the moderate progressive of the group is willing to support change for the good of the people in Middleville. Vatsmeer is especially in favor of change when it will benefit Vatsmeer's own family directly.

5. Queedril Varull, the radical progressive of the town, is very willing to support any change that will move humanity away from the drafty and damp old castle into something more modern and comfortable for humanity.

- Each member of Middleville (classroom) now must chose one of the five positions for humanity to take and support their position with evidence of what they have learned about the Middle Ages.

- A vote will then be taken of all peasants and nobles around town to determine whether or not humanity should move on to the next era. The consensus decision of the imaginary citizens of Middleville will determine their own future and the rest of humanity. (In reality, such decisions by people during the Middle Ages were key in deciding whether humans stayed the way they were or progressed to new levels of development.)

Renaissance, Reformation, and Explorations (1400 to 1600)

UNIT 4: TABLE OF CONTENTS

INTRODUCTION

There are in history ever-so-brief moments that explode with new ideas, new ways of expression, and triumphant masterpieces of art. The era of the Renaissance was just such an explosion of new ways of thinking, across Europe and the rest of the world. Rather than trusting in the mystical beliefs and superstitions of the Middle Ages, people of Middle East, Europe, and the world began to restore their trust in human reason. Such major historical changes do not start in isolation. The initial conditions must first be set—sometimes slowly for hundreds of years—before the right moment and the right person begin the change. This movement toward reason started during the Middle Ages. Major writings of ancient Greece and the Muslim Middle East in science, mathematics, and culture were translated from Arabic into Latin under enlightened twelfth-century Christian governments in Spain and Sicily. These new ideas fed the minds of a few brave people who dared to think differently—St. Thomas Aquinas (thirteenth century) and later Martin Luther (sixteenth century) in religion; Copernicus (fifteenth century) and Galileo (sixteenth century) in science; Giotto (fourteenth century) and Leonardo da Vinci (sixteenth century) in art; and Ibn Batutta (fourteenth century) and Columbus (fifteenth century) in exploration. The results of the changes brought by these thinkers were wondrous to behold. They set the model for other explorers of the mind to follow, down to our present era. But as with all periods of innovation and change, the Renaissance came to an end. The momentum of change brought by the era of the Renaissance was not strong enough and wide enough to continue with renewed energy. With complacency came decline and entropy in the Renaissance. Individuals, governments, and religions became resistant to change and wished to return to a more comfortable era when their minds were not challenged by new ideas. This ended the Renaissance.

THEMATIC LESSON PACS

4.1.0   HISTORICAL TIME LINE

4.1.1   A Renaissance History Time Line

- Name Plates: Photocopy six sets of the following fourteen names and items. Cut each name or item into a strip of paper. Place the strips of paper carefully into separate envelopes for each team and label the envelopes "4.1.1 The Renaissance History Time Line," for later use in class.
- Team Power: Break the class into six teams.
- The Envelope: Each team should be given an envelope containing the following random fourteen names from the Renaissance era:
  1. Michelangelo started painting the Sistine Chapel—1508
  2. Columbus discovered America—1492
  3. Count Dracula lived in Transylvania—1460
  4. Machiavelli wrote *The Prince*—1512
  5. Mary, Queen of Scots, beheaded—1586
  6. Martin Luther started the Reformation—1517
  7. English defeated the Spanish Armada—1588
  8. Mayan civilization disappeared—1400
  9. Muslims and Jews expelled from Spain—1492
  10. Beijing, China, the largest city in the world—1500
  11. Incas had the best road system in world—1500
  12. Cheng Ho started to explore the West—1403
  13. Vasco da Gama reached India—1497
  14. Copernicus saw the sun as the center of the solar system—1473
- Team Time Line: The first job of each team is to correctly order the fourteen names and events according to time, with the oldest at the top and the most recent at the bottom. Each student should separately write the correct time line for the Renaissance names and events on a personal sheet of paper for later reference.

- Team Look Up: Once every member of the team has the Renaissance time line on a sheet of paper, each of the fourteen Renaissance names should be divided between members of the team to find out the meaning of each name from their textbook. Once found, the meanings of each Renaissance name can be shared with the members of the team to write on their own time lines.
- Poster Power: On a large piece of paper, each team should construct its own time line for the Renaissance using the fourteen names with descriptions and illustrations to demonstrate the meaning of each name. When finished, these can be presented to the class and displayed on the classroom wall.
- Music Mart: Each team should pick what they think is the most important name or event in the time line and then compose and present a short song or rap about the name or event. When finished, this can be presented to the class for their approval.
- Journal Entry: Have each team member write a short journal entry speculating about what they now know about the development of humans during the Renaissance—from the time line they developed—and possibly the most important things to happen during this era. When finished, students can first share their thoughts with their team and then with the class as a whole for general discussion about what they think are the most important things that happened during the era.

4.2.0 SEPARATING FACT FROM MYTH AND PROPAGANDA

4.2.1 Witchcraft

Have you ever wondered why more women are not found in history books? Between 1450 and 1650 in central Europe, more than 100,000 women—including young girls—were burned at the stake as witches. This mass killing of women did not take place in illiterate Russia or Scandinavia. It also did not take place in the Muslim Middle East. It took place in the center of Renaissance Europe—Italy, France, England, and Germany—where literacy and reason were flourishing. The printing press had just been invented (1454) and one of the first mass publications of a book by the Catholic Church was *Malleus Maleficarum* (The Hammer of the Witches) in 1487. It was a manual on how to catch female witches and kill them. Because of the manual, over 450 females were burned at the stake for being witches between 1510 and 1514, in the small town of Brescia, Italy. Luther called for a reformation of the Church in 1517—but he did not call for an end to the mass killing of women throughout Europe. Any woman who spoke out, acted differently, or looked different was immediately suspected of being a witch. She could not defend herself and there was no escape. Only in towns and states such as Venice, where accusations of witchcraft were banned, were women safe from the witch hunters. Why were there no great female artists, writers, and scientists during the Renaissance in Europe? The answer is clear. The horror of this Renaissance holocaust against women quickly silenced any creative or intellectual thoughts by the female half of Europe (Shlain 1999).

- Quick Scare: Describe what it would be like if someone accused you of being a witch. How would you feel? What would you do?
- Bumper Sticker: Create a bumper sticker that dramatically demonstrates the horror of the witchcraft holocaust against females in Europe during the Renaissance and Reformation.
- Poster Power: Create a poster that strongly protests the burning of females as witches during the Renaissance and Reformation.
- Role Play: With a partner, develop a short skit of a person accusing another of witchcraft and the person being accused of witchcraft. What would they say to each other? How would they react against each other?
- ADV Witchcraft Inquiry #1: Using your library and the Internet, research why people believe in witches. Accusations of witchcraft tend to be nothing more than people finding scapegoats for other problems. Research possible tensions in a society that might need scapegoats and might turn to accusations of witchcraft. When finished, report your findings to your class.
- ADV Witchcraft Inquiry #2: Many of the top scientists and religious leaders of the Renaissance, and later on Luther, Erasmus, and Newton, believed in witches. How could such learned men believe in witches?
- ADV Witchcraft Inquiry #3: Politicians today still regularly practice "witchcraft" accusations, but under different names. People were accused of being "communists" during the 1950s—much as "witches" were accused during the Renaissance. Look to see if you can find more recent examples of political "witchcraft" accusations.

4.2.2   Count Dracula (circa 1460)

Yes, he really did live in a castle in Transylvania (Romania), he looked like the devil, and he loved blood. Bram Stoker—the author of *Dracula*—did not make that up. His real name was Vlad the Impaler (Do not look up the word "impale" in the dictionary until after lunch!) and he led his soldiers against the Muslims in the Balkans. Poor blood-loving Vlad, however, was not a vampire (Shenkman 1993, 193–194).

* Quick Blood: In a short paragraph, describe your favorite vampire movie.
* Map Attack: Locate Transylvania and possibly Count Dracula's castle on a map and calculate the distance from there to your hometown. Find out how much it would cost to fly to Transylvania (Romania) to visit Count Dracula's castle.
* Vampire Art: Draw or paint a picture—from your imagination—of Count Dracula.
* Diary Entry: As an imaginary vampire, write a description of your life, and the joys and sorrows of your life as a vampire.
* ADV Vampire Analysis: Research in your library and on the Internet how a "nice" guy like Vlad the Impaler can be made into one of the major creatures of modern horror mythology.

4.2.3   Here There Be Dragons!

The early European maps of the known world during the thirteenth century had a strange statement: "Here there be dragons!" Were dragons at the edge of the known world? Of course not. But dragons to Europeans were feared mythological creatures that represented the fearful unknown at the edge of the known world. Even the very earliest tale written in English, *Beowulf*, is about a dragon named Grendel who takes great pleasure in eating humans.

On the opposite side of the world, the Chinese revered dragons as good luck symbols. The five-clawed dragon was the special dragon that brought good luck to each emperor of China. Huge, colorful paper dragons would snake through each Chinese village and town as a symbol of good luck at the beginning of each new year.

Both the folk tales of European evil dragons and the folklore of happy Chinese dragons likely originated in the accidental discovery of

Illustration 4.2.3.   *A traditional Five-toed Imperial Chinese Dragon*

dinosaur bones by ancient humans in different parts of the world. As it quite often happens in history, the facts of the sightings of these large prehistoric creatures' remains became exaggerated and soon developed into mythology and fiction.

- Quick Dragon: Close your eyes for a moment. Imagine a dragon. Now write a short description of the dragon you see. Share your description with the class.
- Concept Web: Draw a concept web of a dragon on the board and then see how many different types and names of dragons can be identified by students in the class.
- Art Mart #1: Create a drawing or a painting of a Chinese mythological dragon.
- Art Mart #2: Create a drawing or a painting of a European mythological dragon.
- Quick Skit: In a team of four, create a quick skit in which the conflicting mythologies of Chinese and European dragons come in contact with each other.
- Folklore #1: Find a story of an evil dragon from European folklore and read it.
- Folklore #2: Find a story of a good dragon from Asian folklore and read it.
- Modern Dragons: *Godzilla* and *Jurassic Park* films are modern mythological stories about dinosaurs. In a pair share, briefly discuss whether or not these stories are modern dragon stories, and then share your pair's ideas with the class.

- ADV Inquiry: Why are dragons so popular in mythology? They can be found in virtually every major culture. Research this topic in your library and on the Internet and then share your findings with the class.
- ADV Historical Dilemma: European dragons represent the unknown and evil; Chinese dragons—on the other side of the world—represent good fortune and good luck. How come? Research this topic and then report your findings to the class.

4.3.0 LOCATION AND MOVEMENT

4.3.1 The Shifting Intellectual Center of the World

The major source of new ideas during the Middle Ages (at least between the years 1000 to 1200 C.E.) was the Muslim Middle East—especially the enlightened Abbasid rulers of Baghdad. The Abbasid rulers gathered all the best thinking from ancient Greece, Persia, and India and translated it into Arabic. With the decline of the Abbasids after the Mongol invasion, enlightened and tolerant Christian rulers in Spain and Sicily during the thirteenth century accepted Muslim, Jewish, and Christian scholars into their courts to translate many of these major Arabic intellectual works into Latin. With the new ideas from the Muslim world, Europe slowly began to pull itself out of the Middle Ages. This flowering of new ideas became especially noticeable in the city-states of Italy—Florence, Venice, and Milan—and began the intellectual, cultural, and artistic garden known as the *Renaissance*.

- Map Think: On a blank map of the world, trace the movement of the intellectual centers of the world between 1000 and 1500.
- What If?: What would have happened if the Muslim intellectuals in Baghdad had not collected the major learning of the ancient Greeks? And what if these works had not been translated into Latin from Arabic? Would there ever have been a European Renaissance? Discuss these issues first in pair shares for one minute each and then share each pair's ideas with the class as a whole.
- Poster Power: Create a poster that illustrates the shift of intellectual thinking from the Muslim Middle East, through Spain and Sicily, into Europe.
- Quick Skit: In a team of four, create a short drama that illustrates the shift of new ideas from the Middle East to Europe during the Middle Ages.

- The King's Scribe: As the official scribe for King Alfonso X of Toledo in Spain, send out an advertisement for Muslim and Jewish scholars to work on translating important scientific works from Arabic into Latin.
- ADV Research: Using the resources in your library and on the Internet, research the impact that the Crusades and Christian attacks on the Muslims in the Middle East had on the transfer of important scientific works from Arabic into Latin during the Middle Ages.
- ADV Question from the Future: Does the world have an intellectual capital today? If so, where would it be? If not, what are the major centers of learning today in the world? Discuss this issue first in a pair share and then in a general class discussion.
- ADV Question from the Future: Are the inventions and technologies of today strong enough to protect the world from losing valuable learning? Interview teachers, parents, neighbors, and friends to learn their views on this issue and report your findings to the class.

4.3.2   Timbuktu in 1492

Timbuktu (in modern Mali) in 1492 was the major commercial and intellectual center in West Africa. Camel caravans from Marrakesh, Morocco, and Algeria would bring blocks of salt south to trade for grain and gold. To travel by camel across the Sahara desert took 114 days. The gold from the Akan mines (in modern Ghana), 600 miles south of Timbuktu, supplied the gold to the countries of Europe and the Mediterranean during the Middle Ages and Renaissance. In exchange, blocks of salt and luxury goods were traded south. The strategic location of Timbuktu at the northernmost point of the Niger River and in the middle of West Africa made it a major trading center and the richest city in West Africa. It also became the major Muslim intellectual center for teaching the Koran and converting much of West Africa to Islam (see Ajayi and Espie 1965).

Note from the Future: The Portuguese explorations along the West African coast in the early 1400s made the old camel caravans across the Sahara obsolete. The merchants of Timbuktu and the Sahara middlemen were cut out of the gold trade as the Portuguese could now make the trip shorter, cheaper, and safer by sea. After 1500 C.E., Timbuktu faded as the major focus of history in West Africa.

- Map Attack: On a blank map of Africa, trace the major trade route across the Sahara Desert from Marrakesh, Morocco, to Timbuktu in modern Mali. How far is it between the two trade centers? If it took

114 days to travel one way between the two places, how many miles did they travel each day by camel? Also indicate how the Portuguese cut off this trade route between Europe and the gold fields in Ghana during the early 1400s.

- You Were There: Imagine pulling a camel for 114 days south across the Sahara Desert and then turning around and making the same trip again to the north. With three other camel drivers (from class), create a short skit describing the rigors of crossing the Sahara.
- Plan a Camel Caravan: Imagine the value of a camel caravan with 200 camels loaded with gold, water, and supplies traveling north across the Sahara. Plan a trip from Timbuktu to Marrakesh for 50 merchants, 100 armed guards, 200 camels and their drivers, and all the food and water for 114 days.
- Meet a Tuareg: Fierce veiled men on camels called Tuaregs controlled much of the central Sahara Desert and demanded payment from any caravan passing through their territory. The favorite saying of the Tuareg was "Kiss the hand you cannot sever!" For one minute each, discuss with a partner in class what you will do when you meet a strong group of Tuaregs riding toward your caravan. When finished, share your ideas with the rest of the caravan (the class).
- Art Mart: Paint or draw a picture of a large camel caravan arriving in Timbuktu from the north after crossing the Sahara Desert.
- Diary Entry: Enter into your diary what it was like to be a member of a trading company crossing the Sahara Desert from Morocco to Timbuktu for 114 days on top of a camel.
- ADV Historical Research: Using your library and the Internet as sources, find out exactly what happened to the camel caravans and Timbuktu once the Portuguese began to bypass the arduous trans-Saharan trips. Be sure to tell your class what you found.

4.3.3 The World's Largest Cities in 1500 C.E.

The following are the important cities of the world in 1500 (Manley 1992, 33–34):

1. Rome in 1500 only had 100,000 people. (During the classic Roman Empire—300 C.E.—Rome held 1.5 million people.)
2. Istanbul (old Constantinople), the capital of the Muslim Ottoman Empire (in modern Turkey), had between 200,000 and 400,000 people.

3. Damascus (in modern Syria), one of the oldest cities in the world, had 57,000 people in 1500.
4. The most important city in ancient Greece—Athens—had only 12,500 people in 1500.
5. Cairo, Egypt, under Muslim Ottoman rule, had 400,000 people in 1500.
6. Viayanager (now Hampi), in India, had a population of 500,000 people, with a circumference of ninety kilometers (sixty miles) in 1500.
7. Tenochtitlan (Mexico City)—the capital of the Aztecs—had 150,000 people in the year 1500, before the arrival of the Spaniards.
8. Cuzco, Peru, the capital of the Incan Empire, had 45,000 people in 1500.
9. Beijing, China, had 672,000 people in 1500.
10. London, England, in 1500, had 60,000 people.
11. Madrid, Spain, was just a small village in 1500.

- Rank Order: Rank order the largest to the smallest city on the list for the year 1500.
- Map It: Locate all of the cities on a blank map of the world and list the size of each city next to its name.
- Analysis: Looking at a map of the major cities of the world on a map of 1500 (the one that you have just completed), what geographic factors can you identify with the largest cities of the world? What geographic features can you identify with some of the smallest cities?
- Comparison: In a short report, compare the size of your town today to the major towns in 1500.
- ADV Historical Research: Pick one of these above towns and determine its patterns of growth and decline. What factors led to these major demographic changes?

4.4.0   POLITICS AND LEADERSHIP

4.4.1   The Most Powerful Nation on Earth—1500

Without question, the most powerful nation on planet Earth in 1500 was the Muslim Ottoman Empire in modern Turkey. In 1453, the Ottoman Turks captured ancient Constantinople (modern Istanbul) and formally ended the Christian Byzantine Empire—the last remnant of the Roman Empire. Within a few years, the Ottomans also conquered most of the Middle East, North Africa, the Balkans, and most of Greece. The Byzantine Christian point guard of Europe was no more. Christian Europe, for the first time in a thousand years, was open to attacks from the east. One of the great strengths of the Ottomans, however, was its toleration of the Christians and Jews who accepted Ottoman rule. Many Christians and Jews rose to prominence within this Muslim state. In 1492, when Christians were forcing Jewish and Muslims to flee Spain, the Ottoman Muslims openly invited the refugees—both Jewish and Muslim, many of them skilled craftsmen and scholars—to settle in the Ottoman Empire. These same Jewish and Muslim refugees from Christian intolerance in Spain revitalized the Ottoman Empire and, in turn, helped produce a Muslim Renaissance of culture and scholarship during the sixteenth century in Istanbul (Abercrombie 1988; Manley 1992).

- Quick Map: On a blank map of the Mediterranean, find and label Istanbul (old Constantinople), the capital of the Ottoman Empire. Shade in the different areas conquered by the Ottomans and the flight of the Jews and Muslims fleeing from Spain to Istanbul in 1492.
- You Were There: Interview the following (imaginary) people (from your class) who were present when Constantinople, the capital of the ancient Byzantine Empire, fell to the Ottoman Turks in 1453. Ask them what the final days were like and what their future plans were.
  1. Alexis—a high patriarch in the Greek Orthodox Church
  2. Fatima—the major wife of Mehmed, the new Ottoman sultan
  3. Constanis—a Greek Christian Byzantine who helped defend the large city wall around Constantinople
  4. Sophia—a Greek Christian noblewoman in Constantinople
  5. Ali—one of the first Muslim Turk soldiers in the Ottoman army who ran through the open door in the city wall of Constantinople
  6. Boris—the spy of the Ottomans who secretly opened the door and let the Ottoman troops into Constantinople in 1453
  7. Mehmed the Conquerer—The Ottoman sultan who captured Constantinople from the Byzantines in 1453
  8. Literus—The head librarian of the Byzantine library who just saw the last copies of the many major playwrights and scientists of ancient Greece go up in flames.

- Front Page: With a team of student editors from your class, produce a front-page edition of the *Renaissance Times* newspaper that focuses on the Jewish refugees fleeing the Christians in Spain and becoming major artists and scholars in the Ottoman Empire. Be sure to include interviews with Jewish refugees and ask other Ottoman Muslims about the Jewish contributions to the Empire.
- ADV Historical Research: Using your library and the Internet, research the Ottoman Empire during the sixteenth century and its wide acceptance of other religions. When completed, report your findings to the class.

4.4.2   Lorenzo—*Il Magnifico*

Can there be a good dictator? If so, then that dictator was Lorenzo de Medici (1449–1492). He was one of the richest men in Italy when he became ruler of Florence in 1469—at the amazing age of twenty. He never had any title except "citizen" and ruled Florence through a council of seventy advisors. His rule of the city for twenty-three years was legendary. Through his efforts, he kept the peace between the Italian city-states during his reign. He supported some of the greatest artists of the Renaissance and he loved poetry, literature, and books. He supported some of the first major works to be written in Italian. His library of more than 1,000 hand-copied books was one of the largest during the Renaissance. He was also one of the first to reintroduce the study of ancient Greek and Roman writers. An ardent supporter of the first printing press (1471) in Florence, he quickly had major writers (such as Homer, Dante, and Euripides) published on the printing press. At the same time, he was also a dictator. He allowed no opposition to his rule, but his rule was so well liked by the people of Florence that they gave him the political power of the city as long as he left them prosperous and happy. He was so well liked that the Pope made Lorenzo's son Giovanni a cardinal in the Church at the age of fourteen (Giovanni later became Pope Leo X). Lorenzo was forty-three when he died in 1492 from gout and stomach problems. All of Italy mourned his passing (see Durant 1953, 110–142).

Note from the Future #1: Lorenzo de Medici's art collection today is the core of one of the greatest museums in the world today—the Uffizi Gallery in Florence. His library of a thousand hand-copied books was the major source upon which much of the rebirth of learning in Europe was based.

Note from the Future #2: One problem with great dictators and great kings: their sons are often very weak, if not terrible, rulers. Lorenzo's son Piero de Medici was such a son.

- Quick ID: Write a short paragraph about the most impressive person you ever met and share it with your class.
- Poet's Corner: Write a short poem or rap about Lorenzo the Magnificent.
- What If?: In a group of four students, discuss what would have happened if Lorenzo de Medici had not ruled Florence. Would Florence have been the center of the Renaissance without Lorenzo's benevolent rule? When finished, report your team's conclusions to the class.
- Ace Reporters: As the ace reporters of the *Renaissance Times* newspaper, your class has been granted an audience with Lorenzo de Medici (a member of your class dressed in costume). Each privileged ace reporter should have a minimum of three questions to ask Lorenzo. Be sure to be prompt. Lorenzo does not like people who are late.
- ADV The Futurist: Analyze whether or not a country, such as the United States, allows great leaders, such as Lorenzo de Medici, to rule without opposition. Or should political checks and balances be kept in place to be sure that even great rulers such as Lorenzo do not gain too much power?

4.4.3 Splendid Isolation—The Ming Emperor of China

The Ming emperors of China (1368–1644)—the sons of heaven—lived in splendid isolation behind the walls of their huge imperial palace in Beijing. To the north, the Great Wall of China shielded the Ming rulers and the Chinese from the Mongolians. To the south and east, the ocean shielded China from the outside world. To the west, the Himalayan Mountains provided another tall shield from the rest of the world. For a very brief time, China launched explorations into and across the Indian Ocean to the West under Cheng Ho, but no longer. China truly retreated into splendid isolation behind its many walls.

- Quick Palace: If you were an all-powerful Ming emperor of China during the Renaissance, with all of the wealth of China at your disposal, make a list of everything you would like to do. Cost is no object. Hand the list to your trusted eunuch (a fellow student) and have him or her read your list of wants to the members of your imperial palace (the classroom).

- Home Boy: What if you lived in isolation all of your life by living in the same small town—without any TV, radio, or newspaper? Imagine a stranger suddenly entering your isolated little town. What would this strange person look like to you? How would you feel about this stranger? How would you treat this stranger? With four students, create a short skit that would illustrate what would happen when this stranger came to town.

- Foreign Devils: The Chinese called all foreigners "foreign devils." You are a foreigner visiting China during the Ming Dynasty. Everybody who speaks to you calls you "foreign devil" instead of your real name. Describe, in a short paragraph how you feel as the "foreign devil" and then share your thoughts with your class.

- Analysis: In a pair share, briefly describe—for one minute each— why you think all Chinese called strangers "foreign devils." When finished, share your thoughts with the class.

- ADV Historical Research: Research in the library and on the Internet the impact of China's historical deep distrust of foreigners. What does it do for China's foreign policy? Be sure to report your findings to the class.

- ADV Long-Range Planning: With a partner in class, devise a long-range plan for changing China's basic distrust of foreigners to trust.

4.5.0   SOCIAL AND ECONOMIC LIFE

4.5.1   Play Ball—In 1520 Mexico!

The Aztecs and all of Mesoamerica from Mexico to the Incas in Peru played a ball game called *tlachco*. At the invitation of Montezuma II, the Aztec king, Hernando Cortés attended a game of tlachco in 1520. His description of the game was as follows:

> Their ball is made from gum from a tree which is kneaded together to make it round. The ball is black in color and bounces well. The tlachco ball court is long and narrow with high stone walls on either side and the ends. High at both ends of the court a protruding stone with a small horizontal hole in it serves as the goal. Players can strike the ball with any part of their body, but are penalized if they do not shoot the goal by bouncing the ball off their

side or their bottom. If the ball hits the wall it is considered out of bounds. The winners of a match receive mantels or the honor of being the winners (Manley 1992, 160; Carey 1987, 86–88).

- Quick Ball: A foreigner who has never seen basketball asks you to describe the game to her. Write a short description of basketball for her to understand the game.
- Venn Diagram: Using a Venn diagram, list the ways that basketball and the Aztec tlachco ball game are similar to and different from each other.
- Play Tlachco: Set a box, a basket, or a hoop against a wall and see if you can hit a ball into the basket or hoop with your hip or bottom. Remember you can hit or kick the ball at any time, but your actual shot must be with your hip or bottom. Report to your class on your tlachco game.
- Poster Power: Make a poster advertising an important upcoming tlachco game between two rival Aztec teams in 1520. Illustrate your poster with a star player making a goal shot with his bottom.

Note from the Future: The Spanish conquerors of Mexico and Mesoamerica banned the game of tlachco, as well as everything else that was Aztec, because it was "the work of the devil." They forced the people of Mexico to speak only Spanish and play only Spanish games.

4.5.2 Life as a Galley Slave (1703)

Life during the Renaissance was not all beautiful artwork and parties in the Vatican. For some, life was very harsh. The small city-states of the Renaissance along the Mediterranean were constantly at war with each other. Much of their naval warfare was done with large "battleships," called *galleys,* in which hundreds of slaves pulled oars to make it move. Particularly harsh was the life of a galley slave: 300 slaves in a galley, five to an oar. The huge oars had to be kept in unison and any sign of weakness was met with a whip across a sweaty, naked back. The heads of the slaves were shaved bald and they slept chained to narrow planks of wood. During the day, the slaves were met with the cramped close-ness of 300 sweating bodies and the open wounds from the whips. At night, the galley slaves were met with swarms of lice, cockroaches, and bugs that fed on their sweat and the blood of their wounds. Protestants, common criminals, and unlucky peasants all became galley slaves on these battleships of the Mediterranean Sea for such states of Venice and Genoa (Carey 1987, 193–198).

- Quick Write: Describe how you would feel if you were chained to a giant oar with 300 other slaves and were beaten with a whip if you did not pull in unison with the others.
- Spin, Counter Spin: With a partner from class, describe the beauty of a Renaissance galley being pulled across the water by hundreds of oars and then describe the horrors of the enslaved men underneath pulling the oars.
- Bumper Sticker: Create a Renaissance bumper sticker supporting the plight of the galley slaves.
- Poster Power: Draw a picture of what you think a galley might look like from the viewpoint of a slave.
- Quick Skit: With four classmates, create a small skit depicting what it was like being a galley slave.
- ADV Historical Research: Search your library and the Internet for more information on slave galleys of the Renaissance and report your findings to the class.

Illustration 4.5.2.   *Drawing of a Venetian Slave Galley, circa 1500*

4.5.3   The Execution of Mary, Queen of Scots (8 February 1586)

The long rule of Elizabeth I, the Protestant queen of England, was not very peaceful. The Protestants and Catholics were constantly at war with each other. Mary Stuart, Queen of Scots, was Elizabeth's cousin, a Catholic, and queen of England—if Elizabeth died. Mary was tricked into supporting a plot to assassinate Elizabeth and was quickly executed for treason. We have a description of her last moments of life:

> Her prayers being ended, the executioners, kneeling, desired her Grace to forgive them her death. She answered: " I forgive you with all my heart." She never changed her countenance and continued to smile to all. With a Corpus Christi cloth pinned around her head to cover her face, the Queen knelt down upon the cushion and spake aloud a Psalm in Latin as she laid her head upon the block. She quickly endured two strokes with the axe. The executioner then lifted her head to the view of all the assembly and stated in a loud voice: "God save the Queen." (Carey 1987, 136–138)

- Quick Death: Write a short paragraph describing why you support or oppose the death penalty.
- Pair Share: With a partner, make a list of all the possible reasons why people have been executed and share this list with the class. As a class, make a larger list.
- Free Verse: Write a short poem describing the death of Mary, Queen of Scots.
- Viewpoint #1: As an English Catholic supporter of Mary, describe your feelings about her execution.
- Viewpoint #2: As an English Protestant supporter of Queen Elizabeth, describe your feelings about Mary's execution.
- Viewpoint #3: As James I, the next king of England, describe your feelings as your mother, Mary, is executed by your aunt, Queen Elizabeth I, for treason (under false pretenses).
- Role Play: As an important team of four lawyers (solicitors) during the reign of Elizabeth, write an opinion of Mary's trial for treason. She was arrested without any reason stated. She was given no lawyer. She was given no opportunity to defend herself. She was given no opportunity to appeal her death penalty. Your team must present a case either for or against her execution for treason.

4.5.4   Incan Medicine and Surgery

Before the invasion of the Americas by the Spaniards, the Incas could
well have been among the best medical doctors in the world. They used
a wide variety of plants and herbs for their medical practice—many of
which are still used today in medicine, such as quinine. They also performed brain surgery, from which people survived and lived many
years afterward. The Spanish, when they conquered Peru, viewed everything the traditional Inca did as evil, and tried to stamp out traditional
Incan medical practices. As a result, much of early Incan medicine was
lost (Manley 1992, 47).

* Quick List: Make a list of all the plants you know that are used for
  medical purposes. Share this list with your class.
* You Were There: As the talk show host for the "You Were There" television show, interview the following on the subject of traditional Incan medicine. Be sure that each member of your studio audience has
  a minimum of three questions to ask our guests about traditional Incan medicine.
  1. De Las Vegas—a Spanish conqueror who thinks that only Euro-
     peans know anything about medicine
  2. Ignadio—a Spanish priest who thinks that the Incas are devil wor-
     shipers
  3. Qsquo—an Incan brain surgeon who has performed over one hun-
     dred successful operations
  4. Atalqua—a traditional Incan herbal doctor whose vast knowledge
     of the use of medicinal plants has saved thousands of lives
* Newspaper Editor: As the editor of the *Renaissance Times* newspaper, write an editorial critical of the Spanish for rejecting Incan medical practices.
* ADV Historical Analysis: Using resources in your library and on the
  Internet, try to find out more on the loss of traditional Incan medicine
  after the Spanish conquest.

4.5.5   Pharmacy in Fifteenth-Century China

Li Shizhen (1518–1591) was perhaps the most famous medical doctor
in China. During his lifetime, he compiled 11,000 prescriptions of different medical substances and the properties of each. His book is still
used today by traditional doctors in China (Manley 1992, 43).

- Quick Write: Who is the most famous doctor you know? Write a short paragraph about this doctor and share it with your class.
- List It: With a partner in class, see how large a list of medicines you can make in a one-minute period. When finished, have each group of partners compare their lists for accuracy and see who has the most number of medicines.
- ADV Historical Research: Check your library or the Internet to see how much influence Chinese medicine has had on the development of Western medicine and report your findings to the class.

4.5.6 Money, Money, Money

We all know and recognize paper money and gold, copper, and silver coins. What else can be used for money? One of the oldest currencies in the world is the cowry shell. Cowry shells come from the Maldive Islands in the Indian Ocean and the Philippine Islands, and have been used as units of currency throughout the world almost since the beginning of recorded history. Ancient Egyptian tombs contain cowry shells. Early Anglo-Saxon gravesites contained them. The earliest tombs in China, India, and the Middle East also contained cowry shells (Manley 1992, 88).

- Quick List: In one minute, make a list of all the different things that might be used for money and share it with your class.
- What if?: What if you did not have any money? What would you do? With a partner, discuss for one minute each of the different techniques you would use to acquire things you wanted without money. When finished, share your ideas with your class.
- Create Money: Money is defined as something with a trusted constant unit of value—something that people can trade, but know that it is always worth the same amount all the time. With a team of four, create a new type of money and then propose it to the class.
- Map Attack: On a blank map of the world and using an atlas, illustrate where cowry shells came from and how they must have traveled to reach ancient Egypt and ancient England thousands of years ago.
- Why Cowries?: In groups of four, discuss the features of cowry shells that made it an ideal international currency in ancient times, as well as the Renaissance, in many places of the world.

- ADV Other Money?: Research your library and the Internet to discover what other items have been used as money across the world and throughout history. When finished, report your findings to the class.
- ADV The Futurist: In a brief essay, speculate what kind of money we can expect to see in the future.

4.6.0   RELIGIOUS THOUGHT

4.6.1   The Renaissance Popes—Alexander VI and Leo X

Never was there such magnificent church art as that made during the Renaissance—and never was there more corruption, fraud, and worldliness in the Church as during the Renaissance. Rodrigo Borgia (1431–1501) and Giovanni de Medici (1475–1521) became true Renaissance popes. In 1492, Rodrigo became Pope Alexander VI and used the papacy as a position of power rather than religious leadership. He openly sold Church positions for money and bribed political and religious leaders for the political advantage of the Church. He openly recognized his mistresses and his two children—Caesar and Lucretia. Popes were not supposed to have mistresses, wives, or children, but that did not seem to bother Alexander VI.

Giovanni became Pope Leo X in 1513. He was the son of Lorenzo de Medici; through his father's wealth and power, he became a church cardinal at the age of fourteen and a pope at the unheard of age of thirty-seven. Leo, like his father, loved art, music, and laughter. Under Leo, musicians played and jesters performed at Church functions. The Pope even played cards with the cardinals of the Church. But Leo was also an intellectual and supported the revival of educating about the ancient (non-Christians) Greeks, such as Plato and Aristotle. The Vatican was obviously the best place to be to have a good time, but was this any way for the leader of the Christian Church to act (see Durant 1953, 404–440)?

- Quick Write: In a short paragraph describe how you think a major religious leader should act.
- Quick Drama: With a group of four students, create a short skit that dramatizes what the Church in Rome was like under Popes Alexander VI and Leo X.

- You Were There: As the host of the popular television program "You Were There," interview the following guests (students) on the topic of the Renaissance popes:

  1. Pietro—a pious Italian pilgrim who has come to the Vatican in Rome to be blessed by the pope.

  2. Nicholi—a Catholic Renaissance priest who thinks that it is important for Christians to have a good time and enjoy the fruits that God has given us on earth.

  3. Johann—a German priest who thinks that it is sinful for Christians to have fun with earthly things such as art, music, and dance.

  4. Lucretia—daughter of Pope Alexander VI and firm believer that the Church should support art and the joy of living.

- ADV Research Question: From a historical perspective, was it more important to have the Renaissance popes be major supporters of the great art works of Michelangelo and others in literature and music or to continue the pious iconoclastic Christianity of the Middle Ages?

4.6.2   The Revolt of the German Churches—1517

A minor German monk by the name of Martin Luther (1483–1546) made a pilgrimage to Rome to visit the Holy City—the Vatican. Rather than feeling holy, he was shocked by what he saw. The offerings he had been collecting from his poor worshipers in Germany were being used to build the largest church in the world, with expensive marble, solid gold statues, jewels, and magnificent paintings and frescos by the Renaissance masters such as Michelangelo. He returned to Germany angry at what he saw. In his anger, in 1517, he nailed "Ninety-five Theses" on the door of his church at Wittenberg in Germany. These were ninety-five reforms he believed the Church in Rome should make in order to return to the simple Christianity he saw being practiced in the Bible. If left alone, Luther would certainly have been burned at the stake for heresy, but several princes from northern German states were tired of Roman rule and willingly hid him and protected him.

- Quick List: With a partner in class, make a list of things that irritate you about your school and tape this list to your classroom door.
- Historical Analysis: From the reading above, list the major things that Luther did not like about the practices of the popes in Rome.

- Rumper Sticker: Create a Renaissance rumper sticker for horses supporting either the Renaissance popes or Martin Luther.
- Poster Power: Draw a picture of Martin Luther nailing his Ninety-five Theses on the church door in 1517.
- ADV Historical Analysis: Why are the Ninety-five Theses of Martin Luther one of the important turning points in world history? Research your library and the Internet for answers to this question. When finished, report your findings to the class.
- ADV Venn Diagram: Compare the Christianity of the early Middle Ages and the Christianity practiced by the Renaissance popes, noting the similarities and differences.
- ADV Research Problem: What were the major historical influences from the Middle Ages and earlier that influenced the Protestant rebellion of Luther and the northern German churches? Research your library and the Internet to find the answer to this question.

4.6.3   The Preliminary Conditions of the Reformation

Major revolutions do not happen in isolation. The background to any revolution is plowed before the seeds of revolution are planted. This is certainly true with the Reformation. Italy during the Middle Ages controlled the religion and much of the wealth of Europe. By 1517, this was rapidly changing (Durant 1957, 332–333).

1. People, not just the priests, were learning to read.
2. People started reading the Bible on their own.
3. People started to think on their own, and not listen to the priests.
4. People started reading the ancient non-Christian Greeks—Homer, Aristotle, and Plato—once again.
5. New ideas of science and mathematics from the Muslim intellectuals were being read.
6. New scientific ideas by Copernicus and others questioned the thinking of the Church.
7. Erasmus (1466–1536) and the other humanist thinkers were quietly and intellectually pushing the Church to reform.
8. The new printing press rapidly spread revolutionary ideas.
9. The rulers and priests in Germany were angry at seeing money earned in their states being sent to Rome to build rich palaces and churches.

10. The Muslims now controlled the eastern Mediterranean after the Crusades, cutting off Italy from the spices and silks of India and China.
11. The Portuguese now sailed directly to India around Africa, by-passing the Italian middlemen and thereby offering cheaper prices for spices and silks.
12. The northern German merchants now traded with the Portuguese, not the Italians.

- Concept Web: Using "Preconditions for the Reformation" as the center, map a concept web of the factors leading to the Reformation.
- Mural Power: Divide each of the preliminary conditions leading to the Reformation among the members of the class and have them illustrate and label their specific preliminary condition and present it to the class. These preliminary conditions can then be displayed along the classroom wall.
- Map Attack: On a blank map of the world, trace the changes in trade routes in 1517 that benefited the Portuguese and Germans but not the Italians.
- ADV Essay: Pull the major preconditions for the Reformation together and describe each precondition as a piece of wood feeding a fire—the fire of revolution.
- ADV Research: Compare the preconditions of the Reformation to other revolutions in history. How are they similar? How are they different? Use your library and the Internet for sources of information on this question.

4.6.4   The Success of the Protestant Revolt

Luther's key pronouncement (1520) was that every person had the right to interpret God and the Bible according to his own judgment. This concept of "free will" was a major change from the medieval Catholic Church. Suddenly, everyone could read the Bible and make up his or her own mind about God. Luther translated the Bible into the language of the people—German. Other reformers did the same in other languages. Intellectuals such as Erasmus and churchmen, even in Italy, read and watched Luther with great interest. The new invention of the printing press rapidly spread every pamphlet of Luther's across Europe. The princes of northern Europe and Germany quickly lined up behind

Luther against the pope in Rome. As his success grew, Luther became more dogmatic and personal rather than just pushing for religious reform. He forgot his early pronouncement of "free will" and began to see his own views as superior to everyone else's—except for those of angels. His attacks against his opponents (Catholics and Jews) became even more vicious toward the end of his life. Although the political leaders of northern Europe stayed with Luther politically, many of his early supporters left him and stayed within the Catholic Church (Durant 1957, 420–437).

- Quick Write: Imagine you are a candidate for the United States Congress. How would you ensure that the people going to the polls would vote for you and continue to support you? Make a list of things you would do to guarantee your reelection and share it with the class.
- Pair Share: With a partner, discuss the basic issue of the Reformation: Does an individual have the "free will" to have personal views about God, or does a religious leader such as the pope have the right to say how we should think about God? Share your pair's views with the class.
- Political Analysis: In teams of four, discuss how a political candidate can win an election: by stating radical views and stating what you think or by taking a more moderate position to gain more supporters? Share your team's views with the class.
- ADV Research: Could Luther have been more successful as a moderate in working to reform the whole Catholic Church (such as Erasmus tried) or did he reach his maximum success as the radical leader of the breakaway Protestant churches? Use sources in your library and on the Internet for information.
- ADV Research: Compare the results of other radicals and other moderates in history to see which ones have been more successful at bringing about needed change.

4.6.5   Erasmus (1466–1536)—The Middle Position

Erasmus—the rationalist of the Reformation—had openly called for Church reform in his book *In Praise of Folly* long before Luther. Luther read the works of Erasmus and used many of his thoughts in his Ninety-Five Theses. Erasmus, in turn, strongly supported Luther's initial criticism of Church practices in 1517, but Erasmus was openly critical of Luther when he later changed to openly attack the pope himself and the whole Church.

In a letter to Luther in 1519, Erasmus wrote:

> I confine myself to literature as far as I can, and keep aloof from other quarrels, but generally I think courtesy to opponents is more effective than violence. It might be wiser of you to denounce those who misuse the Pope's authority than to censure the Pope himself. So also with kings and princes. Old institutions cannot be rooted up in an instant. Quiet argument may do more than wholesale condemnation. Avoid all appearance of sedition. Keep cool. Do not hate anybody. Do not be excited over the noise you have made. (Durant 1957)

Luther rejected Erasmus as a weak Catholic and continued to directly attack the pope. The Catholics, in turn, distrusted Erasmus and accused him of being a secret Lutheran. Erasmus wanted reason, not emotion, to rule. Afraid for his life—from both sides—Erasmus fled to Basel, Switzerland, where he could continue his intellectual life of the Renaissance. In Switzerland, he was safe from the bloodshed of the coming Thirty Years War fought between the Catholics and the Protestants (Durant 1957, 427–437).

- Quick Write: Describe in a short paragraph a time in your life when two friends were arguing and you refused to take either side. In return, they were both angry with you.
- Quick Draw: Draw a picture of Erasmus struggling to maintain a reasonable neutral position in the fight between the Protestants and Catholics and share it with your class.
- Pair Share: With a partner in class, discuss why you think Erasmus risked his life to steadily maintain a neutral position in the Reformation? When finished, share your ideas with the class.
- ADV Historical Analysis: Look through history to identify other individuals who worked hard to maintain neutral positions during major struggles or issues. What was the result of their struggles?
- ADV Take a Stand: Pick a major hot issue of today. Define both the pro and con positions of each side and then describe a neutral position between both sides. Now decide which position you will take and describe why you have picked this position.
- ADV Position Analysis: Is it often harder to take a neutral position on some issues than to go along with the crowd and either support or

attack something? Write a short position statement on this topic and share it with your class.

4.6.6   The Failed Compromise of Ratisbon in 1541

Pope Leo X and many of the popes after him did not understand Luther's Protestant Reformation. They thought it was just a religious quarrel between German monks, and they were more interested in the joyful delights of the Renaissance. The reality of the Reformation came home to the Church leaders when a large irregular army of German Protestants attacked and sacked Rome in 1527. Cardinals and leaders began to reform the excesses of the Renaissance popes and looked for ways to compromise with the Lutherans. Leading Protestants and Catholics met in 1541 in the town of Ratisbon in the Alps to work out a compromise. They agreed to compromise on everything, except on the power of the pope to change wine into the blood of Christ during communion—and the compromise failed. On this seemingly small point of theology, the Protestant and the Catholic churches permanently split and went their separate ways (Durant 1957, 921–933).

Note from the Future: The real struggle that Luther started in 1517 was not between the Renaissance and the Reformation. It was Luther's desire to return to the deep religious faith of the Middle Ages and his opposition to the still-developing Enlightenment that focused on individual freedom, political rights, religious freedom, and scientific thought, and which would fully emerge after 1600.

- Quick Write: Describe an instance in your life when you and a friend or family member failed to reach an agreement in an argument. What was the precise thing on which you disagreed? On reflection, could you now reach a compromise on this issue? Share your reflections with the class.
- You Were There: As the host of this popular TV talk show, conduct an imaginary interview of the Protestant and Catholic theologians (students) who attended the Ratisbon Conference in 1541. Quiz them on why they failed to reach a compromise, which resulted in a divided Europe. Could these (student) theologians reach a compromise now?
- ADV Research #1: Examine the records of history for other conferences that failed to reach compromises and resulted in major fight-

ing. Use the resources in your library and the Internet to research this topic.

- ADV Research #2: Using your library and the Internet, compare the clashes throughout history between the faithful of one religious belief and those who wish to have the freedom to reason and believe in their own ways.

4.7.0 CONQUEST AND WARFARE

4.7.1 Joan of Arc

Warfare during the Renaissance was rather strange, with bands of hired thugs (*condottieri*) fighting for whoever paid the most. Perhaps the strangest war during this period was the Hundred Years War (1337–1453), which, of course, did not last 100 years. Subtract and you will come up with 116 years.

Even stranger was a young teenager during the Hundred Years War named Joan of Arc. Her actions during this strange war stirred the patriotic spirit in Frenchmen and she (much later in history) became the symbol of France with her own statue in Paris. Joan was a teenage girl who dressed in boys' clothes and heard voices from God. In most other instances, she would have been quickly locked up. She was, however, given the task of leading the French army during several battles during the Hundred Years War. She amazingly won a couple of battles, but then was captured and burned at the stake by the English for being a witch (Shenkman 1993, 49–50, 143–145).

- Quick Write: Make up your own story of a symbol or hero of your own imaginary country and share it with the class.
- Historical Question: With a partner in class, discuss why would someone call a war the Hundred Years War when it really lasted 116 years. When finished, share your ideas with the whole class. Are there other such misnamed wars and events in history?
- Newspaper Reporter #1: As the top reporter of the *Renaissance Times* newspaper, write up your recent (imaginary) interview with Joan of Arc for a front-page feature article and format it on a word processor.
- Newspaper Reporter #2: As the military analyst for the *Renaissance Times* newspaper, report on your interview (imaginary) with

the French military general who picked Joan of Arc to lead his army.

- Question from the Future: What would happen today with a general who picked a young teenage girl to lead his army?

4.7.2   Agincourt (25 October 1415)

Jehan de Wavrin, a French knight, gave his eyewitness account to one of the major battles of the Hundred Years War—Agincourt. Ten thousand English archers and knights under Henry V met 50,000 French knights in full armor. It rained all night in the narrow, boggy field of Agincourt. Two forward battle lines of English archers–armed with powerful long bows—rained arrows down on the tightly packed French knights mounted on horseback in full armor and banners. The fully armored French knights were so heavy their horses quickly became mired in the mud and could not move. The English arrows continued to rain down on the French, wounding horses and knights alike, but they could not move forward into the English arrows or backward into the field of thousands of knights behind them. Out of arrows, the English forces advanced with axe and broadsword to kill or capture all the knights wounded or stuck in the mud. The rest of the French army fled the battlefield (Carey 1987, 68–76).

Note from the Future: The battle was one of the greatest in English history and became a battle cry for the English during wartime. Shakespeare's play *Henry V* and Sir Lawrence Olivier's World War II film *Henry V* focused on the Battle of Agincourt.

- Quick Write: Describe a game your school has played in which everybody imagined that you would lose, but you really finally won. How do you feel?
- Quick Skit: In teams of four students each, write and dramatize a short skit of the Battle of Agincourt. Divide up the class and have half of the teams creating skits from the English point of view and the other half of the teams from the French point of view.
- Art Mart: Draw a picture of the Battle of Agincourt depicting the English long bowmen against the fully armored French knights on horseback.
- Spectator: As a spectator watching the epic Battle of Agincourt from a hidden spot in the woods, describe what you saw in a short article for the *Renaissance Times* newspaper.

- ADV Historical Research: Why do humans so often take such great pride in battles they have won and the great numbers of people they have killed?

4.7.3   The Spanish Armada (1588)

Phillip II of Spain was fuming mad with Elizabeth I of England. He was Catholic and she was Protestant. She refused his proposal of marriage. Elizabeth's father, Henry VIII, never paid back the immense dowry when he divorced Phillip's sister, Catherine of Aragon. Elizabeth had also just beheaded Mary, Queen of Scots—her cousin, a Catholic, and next in line to be queen of England. Phillip's answer was to invade England. He gathered 130 ships from Portugal, Venice, and the Vatican to attack. Elizabeth had spies everywhere and knew long in advance of the Spanish plans. She gathered 197 ships under Sir Francis Drake and waited. The tall Portuguese galleons were slow, heavy, and did not sail well when going upwind. The prevailing winds blew south from England to Spain, making it very hard to sail. After a few small clashes, Drake sent a flaming ship into the tightly packed Spanish fleet, scattering them. A large storm came up, pushing the Spanish fleet north to Scotland. Sailing around Scotland, many of the Mediterranean galleys—veterans of Lepanto—did not sail well in the rough seas of the open Atlantic and sank. Others crashed into Ireland—the Spanish maps did not have the location of Ireland marked correctly on their maps. Most of the large, old Portuguese galleons got home safely, but England proclaimed a great victory over the Spanish (Shenkman 1993, 119–122).

- Quick Cheer: As the leader of an English cheering squad, develop and present to your class a cheer for the English before the battle with the Spanish Armada.
- Counter Cheer: As the leader of a Spanish cheering squad, develop and present to your class a cheer for the Spanish *after* the battle of the English fleet (even though you did not do so well in the battle).
- Map Attack: On a blank map of Europe, mark the major movements of the Spanish Armada during the attempted invasion of England. Label your map to explain why the Spanish invasion was not successful.

- History or Myth? With a partner in class, discuss whether or not the English were correct to proclaim victory over the Spanish Armada, or did Mother Nature deserve the credit for stopping the invasion force? Explain your answer to the class when finished.
- Eyewitness: As an imaginary eyewitness to the battle with the Spanish Armada of 1588, write a description of the battle from your viewpoint and then share it with the class.
- ADV Research: Using your library and the Internet, find how many "great" battles in history were really won by one army getting lost, a giant storm interrupting the fighting, or a major accident taking place. Report your findings to the class.

4.8.0   TRAGEDY AND DISASTER

4.8.1   The Expulsion of the Jews from Spain in 1492

The new Christian rulers expelled the Jews as well as the Muslims from Spain in 1492. An estimated 300,000 Jews were forced to leave Spain that year, although many remained as nominal Christians. Waves of Jewish expulsions swept Europe during the Middle Ages and the Renaissance; England in 1290 and France in 1394 are specific examples. Often, however, they were quickly invited back. Christians during the Middle Ages and Renaissance believed in the sin of usury, which was making money by charging interest. Jewish merchants and bankers had no such sin as usury. As a result, kings, nobles, and rich Christian merchants needed the Jewish bankers to handle their monetary transactions so that the Church would not punish them. Jewish bankers paid for Columbus's voyages to the New World in 1492, not the jewels of Ferdinand and Isabella. Many former Spanish Jews and Muslims were also quickly accepted by Muslim rulers in Morocco, Turkey, and Egypt, which led to a second Muslim-Jewish Renaissance in the Middle East (Manley 1992, 32).

- Quick Write: Imagine you were a Jew or a Muslim in 1492 being forced to leave your home and your country in Spain by Christian armies. Describe how you would feel. What would you do?
- Ace Reporter: As the hot-shot reporter for the *Renaissance Times* newspaper, write on-the-spot interviews of Muslims and Jews being forced out of Spain and make them feature articles for the next edition of your paper.

- Newspaper Editor: As the editor of the *Renaissance Times* newspaper, write a critical editorial concerning the expulsion.
- Quick Money: "Usury"—making money by charging interest—was a sin for early Christians. With a partner in class, discuss what would happen to the banking system in the United States today if this were still a "sin" for Christians. Share your thoughts with the class when finished.
- ADV Right On #1: What human rights are violated when one set of people expels people from another ethnic group or religion from a country? What actions, if any, should be used to prevent such actions in the future?
- ADV Right On #2: What human rights are violated when one set of people stops people from another ethnic group or religion from *entering* a country? What actions, if any, should be used to prevent such actions in the future?

4.8.2   Disappearance of the Mayan Civilization—1400

Sometime before the European explorers arrived in Central America, the Mayan civilization disappeared back into the heavy rainforests of Central America. The Mayan people were still there, but their powerful city-states with major temples, pyramids, and governments were no longer being used. What happened? Why did such a people with very advanced thinking in mathematics and astronomy disappear? Mayan archaeologists today do not know why. The Mayan city-states were constantly at war with each other near the end—that is one clue. Another clue is that the tropical rainforest soils, as in all of Central America, are not very fertile. The success of the Mayan civilization could have been the cause of its decline. An educated guess might be that too many people trying to farm poor soil led to fighting between cities over new land, overcrowding, and the eventual decline of the Mayans (Manley 1992, 32).

- Quick Write: Describe what happens to a herd of animals when there is too little food and too many animals. Describe several actions that could be used to prevent this situation.
- Poster Power: Make a poster depicting the struggle of the last years of the Mayan civilization. Label the different images in your poster and share it with your class.
- Bumper Sticker: Create a Mayan bumper sticker promoting efforts to save the Mayan civilization.

- Map Attack: Research in the library the location of the major Mayan city-states in Central America; using a map of the area, present your findings to the class.
- ADV Future Research: What problems will the world face if the food supply decreases and the population increases? What actions can be taken to delay or prevent such a tragedy?

4.8.3   Genocide of the Native Populations of the Americas

The eyewitness descriptions of the Spanish atrocities against the native Americans in the Caribbean Sea by the Dominican missionary Bartolomé de las Casas curdle the blood.

> The Spaniards with their horses, spears and lances began to commit murders and strange cruelties as they entered into the towns and villages sparing neither children nor old men nor women with child. They taught their fierce dogs to tear them to pieces at first view. In my presence without cause I saw three thousand souls—men, women and children—put to the edge of the sword without cause what so ever. I saw there such great cruelties, that never any man living either have or shall see the like. (Carey 1987, 82–84)

The Spaniards also carried the deadly disease of smallpox to the Americas and effectively wiped out most of the native population of the Caribbean islands and the Americas. A major factor in the success of the Spanish conquests of the Aztecs in Mexico and Incas in Peru was smallpox. The Spanish attacked both peoples during raging epidemics of smallpox, which left these American empires powerless to stop the small Spanish armies. The combined Spanish atrocities and epidemics of European diseases rapidly wiped out most of the native peoples of the Caribbean and the Americas. An estimated population of Mexico in 1500 was 25 million; by 1600, the native population of Mexico was one million people (McNeil 1977, 183–190).

- Quick Write: Describe what happens when someone in your family gets a bad cold or the flu. Imagine in a short paragraph what would happen if this were a major unknown disease that was killing people across the nation.
- You Were There: As the host of this popular TV show, interview the following eyewitnesses (students in costume) to the Spanish conquest of the Americas:

1. Atahulpa—the Inca Emperor who died of small pox during the Spanish conquest
2. Montezuma II—the Aztec emperor who was stabbed to death by the Spanish during the Spanish attack
3. Pizzaro—the leader of the Spanish attack against the Incas
4. Cortez—the leader of the Spanish conquest of Mexico
5. Malenche—the young native woman who aided Cortez by serving as his translator and spy against the Aztecs

- ADV Today #1: For class discussion, if a group, like the Spanish in 1519, attempted to eliminate an ethnic group today, what actions could be taken by the rest of the world to stop such inhumanity?
- ADV Today #2: For class discussion, should the United States and other countries in the world have the right to develop and use biological weapons as deadly diseases in warfare? What can be done to prevent this from happening?

4.8.4   The Dreaded Spanish Inquisition

In 1622, William Lithgow, an Englishman, was brought before the Inquisition in Spain and charged with heresy against the Church. In order to force a confession from him, he was placed on the dreaded rack and tortured. Amazingly, he survived the ordeal and later wrote a description of his experience.

> I was brought to the rack, then mounted on the top of it. My legs were drawn through the two sides of the three-planked rack. A chord was tied about my ankles. As the levers bent forward, the main force of my knees against the two planks burst asunder the sinews of my hams, and the lids of my knees were crushed. My eyes began to startle, my mouth to foam and froth, and my teeth to chatter like the doubling of a drummer's sticks. My lips were shivering, my groans were vehement, and blood sprang from my arms, broken sinews, hands and knees. Being loosened from these pinnacles of pain, I was hand-fast set on the floor, with this incessant importation: "Confess! Confess!" (Bronowski 1973)

- Quick Write: Why do some people in power—now and throughout history—think they have the authority to torture people? Write a short paragraph on your views of this question.
- Poster Power: Create a poster that illustrates your views on human torture.

- Pro and Con: In teams of four, discuss the problem of a historical organization such as the Church that wants to make sure its members follow an established set of beliefs. Is it better for such an organization to force members to follow a set range of beliefs or is it better for the organization to convince members by reasonable argument to follow a set of beliefs? Each team should then present its views to the class for full discussion.
- ADV Action Research: Student teams of four members each should contact Amnesty International for information concerning governments and organizations that are still torturing people today, and then report to the class on what they found.
- ADV Historical Research: Using the library and the Internet, research the history of the Inquisition of the Catholic Church, and find out the opinion of the Church today regarding this dark page in its history. Be sure to report your findings to the class.

4.9.0   EXPLORATION AND DISCOVERY

4.9.1   Why Not the Vikings?

Why did the Vikings not get credit for discovering America? In 986 C.E., a Norwegian, Bijarni Herjolfsson, mistakenly sailed past Greenland and landed in modern day Labrador in Canada. In 1000 C.E., Leif Eriksson took Herjolfsson's boat further south to Newfoundland, where the Vikings later founded a settlement. These discoveries of America were a full 500 years before Columbus. Why did they not get credit for these discoveries?

The answer is simple: communication. The Vikings of 1000 did not know how to read or write, and were not on very friendly terms with the rest of Europe. Viking ships were constantly attacking the communities of Europe along the coast. Western Europe had no strong governments; the only strong states at the time were the Byzantine Empire in modern Turkey and the Islamic Empire in Baghdad, and these two powerful states were more interested in the Silk Road to the east and certainly had no interest in lands to the west of Greenland (Manley 1992, 62).

- Quick Discovery: If you were the first to discover something new in science or in space, how would you advertise it to the world?
- Poster Power: Make a poster illustrating the Viking discovery of North America.

- Bumper Sticker: Make a bumper sticker concerning the Viking discovery of America.
- Madison Avenue: As the top four salespeople (students) of the Viking Advertising Company, develop a hot ad campaign to promote the Viking discovery with jingles, thirty-second prime-time TV ads, and a junk mail blitz. When finished, present your ad campaign to your class for their approval.
- ADV Historical Analysis: Compare the reasons why the world knew little, if anything, about the Viking discoveries yet knew within a year the discoveries of Columbus in 1492.

4.9.2 Zeng He (Cheng Ho)—The Great Chinese Explorer (1405–1433)

Between 1405 and 1433, the Chinese emperor's grand eunuch, Cheng Ho, conducted major explorations by sea to the east across the Indian Ocean. His great fleet of ships contained giant five-masted sailboats over 426 feet (130 meters) in length with as many as five decks. (All three of Columbus's little caravels could have fit on the deck of one of Cheng Ho's junks.) The purpose of Cheng Ho's explorations was to demonstrate China's greatness to the world. Wherever Cheng Ho visited, if the local ruler proclaimed China was the greatest nation in the world, Cheng Ho would then shower the ruler with gifts. The great fleets of Cheng Ho sailed to India and then later down the eastern coast of Africa to modern Mozambique. In 1433, the isolationists came to power in China and retreated behind the great Chinese wall. They strongly opposed Chinese ships going out to contact strange foreigners. Following a seemingly regular theme in Chinese history, this giant nation retreated once again into isolation. They kept Cheng Ho at home and destroyed his great ships (Boorstin 1983).

- Quick Map: On a blank map of the world, trace the route Cheng Ho's Chinese junks traveled in 1433 to "discover" India and East Africa and then trace the route of Columbus's trip to the "New World" in 1492.
- Map Attack: Measure the length of Cheng Ho's voyage of discovery versus Columbus's voyage of discovery. Which is greater in length?
- Pair Share: Discuss with your partner why Columbus is mentioned in every world history textbook and Cheng Ho mentioned in very few textbooks. Share your pair's views with the class.

- Historical Importance: In terms of historical change, which voyage was the more important, that of Columbus or that of Cheng Ho? Support your conclusion in a short essay and present it to your class for comments.
- How Come?: In a pair, share and then in a full class discussion, examine why the European explorers began their expeditions in search of gold and the Chinese began their expedition in search of new countries to whom they could give gifts of gold and silks.
- ADV What if?: In 1433, the fleets of Cheng Ho had already been down the east coast of Africa and were ready to round the Cape of Good Hope into the Atlantic Ocean. What if the Chinese had continued to sail up the west coast of Africa and "discovered" Europe? Hypothesize how that would have changed history.
- ADV Research into the Future: Chinese history is full of cautious contacts with the rest of the world and then rapid reversals to full isolation from the world. The Great Wall, the burning of Cheng Ho's ships, and other such isolationist cycles are a major theme in Chinese history. Use resources in your library and on the Internet to explore this major theme in Chinese history and report your findings to your class (Boorstin 1983).

4.9.3   The Portuguese and Prince Henry

The Portuguese were different from the Spanish. While Spain looked to Italy and the Renaissance, Portugal looked to the Atlantic Ocean with England to the north, and Africa to the south. While Spain supported Columbus on a lucky whim, Portugal carefully planned its explorations step by step for more than 100 years. Portugal also had the ideal man for explorations—Prince Henry the Navigator. He liked the intellectual excitement of exploration, and opened his own school of exploration at Sagres, on the southern most tip of Portugal, shortly after 1415. Mapmakers, navigators, and shipbuilders all came to Sagres to study with Prince Henry. He designed a special ship for exploration—the caravel. It was small, fast, and able to sail tight to the wind with lateen sails. Prince Henry and the Portuguese also did not have the ethnic prejudices of the Spanish. Prince Henry's father was Portuguese and his mother was English. He borrowed much of his caravel's design and sails from the Arabs. His main navigators were Arab and his main mapmakers were Jewish.

His main interest was the coast of Africa. When his ships started to explore down the coast, he did not know that it would become the route to India. The Atlantic coastline of Africa was unknown past Cape Bojador and looked exciting. He sent ships to explore it, and suddenly the world became a larger place (Boorstin 1983, 156–164).

- Quick Write: If you want a new fresh idea, whom do you turn to among your friends? Why do you turn to this friend for new ideas?
- T Chart: Compare the differences between the Portuguese and the Spanish. How did these differences affect the explorations of these two countries?
- Map Attack: On a large map of Africa, find Cape Bojador (off the Western Sahara and south of the Canary Islands), which was the limit of Europe's knowledge of Africa in 1415. On a blank map of Africa, write "unknown" on Africa south of Bojador. On your map, draw in mythological dragons to depict the "unknown" south of Bojador, much as mapmakers did before Prince Henry. Now imagine what may lie beyond the Cape and share your ideas with your class.
- Letter Writer: As an imaginary visitor to Prince Henry's school of navigation, write a letter to a friend describing the excitement of the place.
- ADV Historical Research: New discoveries and explorations do not happen by accident. Someone has the initial ideas to look for something new. Look back in history in your library and on the Internet to find other such people who had new ideas and led the way for further explorations.

4.9.4   Columbus—Who Was He?

We all know the story of the poor weaver's son from Italy who got the support from the queen of Spain and discovered America. It makes a great "poor boy makes good" story—almost mythological—but is it true? Let's look at some recent questions about Columbus to see if the story holds up.

1. We know that Columbus easily and regularly had access to the royal courts of Portugal and Spain, but fifteenth-century Europe had a very tight class society. Royalty and commoners (especially weavers) did not mix. Was Columbus really a poor commoner or was he secretly a member of royalty?

2. Columbus spoke fluently in Spanish and Portuguese, and wrote in an interesting mixture of Portuguese and Spanish, but never in Italian. Was he really Italian?

3. The best navigators of the era attended Prince Henry's navigation school at Sagres in Portugal. Columbus was obviously very good at navigation. Did he secretly attend the school? Only Portuguese navigators attended.

4. Columbus told King Ferdinand and Queen Isabella of Spain that his request for support had been turned down by King John II of Portugal. If so, why did he sail directly to Lisbon and report to the king of Portugal after his first voyage—before he sailed to back to Spain?

Columbus remains a mystery. Was he really who he says he was? Barreto (1992) thinks that Columbus was a secret agent of the Portuguese, who was used to send the Spanish off in another direction— west—and away from Portugal's recently discovered (1486–1487) route to India around Africa. No one realized, however, that there were two unknown continents out west, and Columbus accidentally tripped over them on his way to China. What is the real story about Columbus? We do not know. The truth is out there for us to discover.

- Quick Write: In a short paragraph, describe the story you heard about Columbus in grade school.
- T Chart: Compare the story of Columbus described in a textbook with the story described above. Which sounds more realistic to you? Why?
- Write a Letter: Imagine you lived in 1492 and are really excited by Columbus's recent discovery. Write a letter to him. What would you say? What would you ask him?
- ADV Research: Read three different articles about Columbus from the library and report to the class about your findings.

4.9.5   Why Did Columbus Become So Famous?

What did Columbus do that made him so famous? Answer: His discovery of America was one of the major change points in world history. He had a crazy idea that he could sail west directly to China and India. People laughed at him and called him crazy, but he stuck to his idea. He finally got support from Spain to try it out in three little ships, but he really failed in what he wanted to do. He thought he was in China or India and did not realize he was in the Americas. But wow, for an accident, it was a real discovery! Gold, lots of new foods, lots of new animals, and lots of different people. It opened peoples' eyes and made them realize the world was very different from what they had been taught. It was also the world's first media event. The printing press had just been invented and some of the first news printed was that of Columbus's discoveries. News of Columbus was quickly printed in almost every major European language. For the first time in history, people were excited about something in print and they could not wait for more to come. He had the P.R. (public relations) machine that the Vikings never had.

- Quick Write: Do you think that people who have a different but very interesting idea should stick with it, or listen to people around them who make fun of it?
- Diary Entry: Imagine you are one of the first people in the world to read that Columbus just discovered that you can sail west to reach India and China. How do you feel? What does it mean to you? Write in your diary what his trip meant to you.
- Stern Sticker: Make a stern sticker to stick on the backside of the Santa Maria—the flagship of Columbus.
- Hot Off the Press: Make an imaginary mock-up of the first printed sheet announcing Columbus's new discoveries and share it with your class.
- What If?: What if Columbus never made it to America? Do you think someone else would have found it? Discuss this issue in a pair share and then in a full class plenary session.
- ADV Research: How much luck and how much skill enabled Columbus to accidentally discover the Americas? Use your library and the Internet to research this question and report your findings to the class.

4.9.6 Da Gama's Fast Trip to India in 1497

A young twenty-eight-year-old sailor from Portugal by the name of Vasco da Gama (1469?–1524) made an extraordinary voyage in 1497. Da Gama's trip, however, was not an accidental discovery, such as that by Columbus. For most of the fifteenth century, the Portuguese had slowly and carefully been exploring down the west coast of Africa. The key discovery that enabled da Gama to sail to India was the rounding of the Cape of Good Hope (the southern end of Africa) by Bartholomew Diaz in 1486–1487. The Portuguese were quite excited by the discovery by Diaz. They now knew that they could sail around Africa by ship to reach the rich spices of India and avoid the Arab middlemen. Da Gama's trip was also successful because his was the first voyage of exploration to really understand that the world was round and thereby take advantage of the circular ocean currents. To do so, he was the first to fully use the counterclockwise ocean currents of the south Atlantic. From Portugal, he traveled southwest across the Atlantic and the equator along the coast of Brazil and then followed the currents back to the east across the south Atlantic to the Cape of Good Hope. Sailing up the east coast of Africa to Malindi (in modern Kenya), he hired a Muslim geographer to take him to Calicut (modern Kozhikose) in India. Again following the currents, Da Gama returned to Portugal a rich man with a boatload of pepper and spices from India. In one trip to India, the Portuguese had learned the basic round shape of the world, the shape of its major continents, and the direction of the world's major ocean currents. This one trip by a young Portuguese sailor ended the domination of the Italian city-states, such as Venice, over the trade between Europe and Asia. The monetary advantage enjoyed by Italy and that paid for much of the glories of the Renaissance was now gone (Boorstin 1983, 172–177).

- Quick Write: Think of one small thing you did that really changed your life and describe it to the class.
- Map Attack #1: On a blank map of the world, trace the route of DaGama from Portugal to India and back. Be sure to remember the counter-clockwise ocean currents that Da Gama followed in the south Atlantic.
- Map Attack #2: After plotting Da Gama's route from Portugal to India and back, calculate the length of the trip in miles and kilometers, and then estimate how long the voyage took if his ship traveled approximately 150 miles a day.
- Poster Power: Make a poster to illustrate the immense impact Da Gama's voyage had on Europe and the rest of the world in 1498.
- Music Mart: With a partner, write a short song, poem, or rap about Da Gama's voyage to India and perform it for your class.

- Diary Entry: As a sailor for Da Gama on his voyage to India, make a diary entry describing what it was like to be the first to sail from Europe to India and back.
- ADV Historical Comparison: Compare the voyage of Da Gama with the voyage of Columbus. Which was longer? Which had more immediate economic impact? Which had a longer-range impact?

4.9.7   Was Magellan the First around the World?

The Portuguese navigator Magellan (1480–1541) started his around-the-world expedition from Spain in 1519 with five ships and 270 men. They sailed down the east coast of South America, through the Straits of Magellan, and into the Pacific. They crossed the Pacific. In Malaysia, Magellan died in a small battle in 1521. Juan del Cano (d. 1526), who chronicled the voyage, continued to sail west across the Indian Ocean, then around Africa, and somehow made it back to Spain in 1522 with one battered ship and twenty starving men. This was certainly one of the most amazing trips human beings have ever taken, but the question remains: Who was the first to go round the world? Del Cano—because he completed the trip back to Spain? Magellan because he had already been in Malaysia on another trip? And do not forget Enrique, Magellan's Malaysian slave who had gone around the world with Magellan and stayed in Malaysia when Magellan died (Manley 1992, 64).

- Quick Write: Imagine traveling on a voyage with your friends and you were one of the only ones who returned alive. Describe your feelings in a short paragraph.
- Map Attack: On a blank map of the world, trace the amazing voyage of Magellan.
- Ace Reporter: As the ace reporter of the *Renaissance Times* newspaper, you are on the scene when Del Cano brings his ship into port after returning from around the world. Describe the scene and Del Cano's first impressions of the trip. With your editorial team, make a bold front-page edition of this late-breaking event.
- Chart It: On a chart, compare the expeditions of Columbus, Da Gama, and Magellan. Based on your comparison, which was the most important?
- ADV Research: Find out how sailors managed to survive on early sailing explorations such as Magellan's. What did they eat when their regular food gave out or became rotten?

4.10.0   INVENTION AND REVOLUTION

4.10.1   Copernicus (1473–1543)

The medieval Christian Church believed that the Earth was the center of the universe because humans (God's creations) lived on Earth. To say that is was not true was heresy and a sin, punishable by being burned at the stake. Copernicus, a Polish churchman, discovered that the sun, not the Earth, was the center of our solar system—contrary to the teachings of the Church. For fear of being burned at the stake, Copernicus did not publish his findings until 1473—the year of his death. True to his fears, both the Catholic and Protestant Churches condemned his findings as heresy. Even Martin Luther was bitterly opposed to these new radical ideas of Copernicus. "Such crazy ideas will turn the world upside down," said Luther. In a way, Luther was right; the discoveries of Copernicus completely changed how humans viewed planet Earth. The Church, however, was not ready for such new ideas. Copernicus was declared a heretic and his books were burned; luckily for Copernicus, he died before his book was published (Boorstin 1983).

- Quick Think: Watch the sun, the moon, and the stars as they move across the sky. Make an argument from your direct observations that the Earth, not the sun, is the center of the universe.
- What If?: In a pair share, discuss with a partner: if you made such a gigantic discovery, such as Copernicus had, that was so much against the teachings of the Church, would you hide what you learned, or would you tell everybody your new discovery and be willing to die for what you found?
- Art Mart: Make a drawing or a painting that illustrates the great conceptual change of planet Earth that Copernicus made for human beings.
- Quick Skit: With a team of four students, create a short drama that illustrates the conflict Copernicus faced with the Catholic and Protestant Churches of his day.
- ADV Research: Using your library and the Internet, examine why both Protestant and Catholics—bitter enemies during the Reformation—declared that Copernicus's findings were heresy and had his books burned. Also find out who—if anybody—had the courage to support Copernicus during this period.

- ADV The Futurist: Using resources in your library and on the Internet, research how the Church finally came to accept the discoveries of Copernicus.

4.10.2   The World's Greatest Invention—The Printing Press

One of the greatest inventions of any age was the invention of the printing press. The art of papermaking came into Europe during the Middle Ages from the Muslims in Spain. The art of printing with blocks was invented in China, but the written Chinese language (with more than 50,000 separate characters) was impractical for an early printing press. The invention of carving separate letters and words of a language on moveable blocks, covering them with ink, and then printing them on paper was an invention by Laurens Janszoon Coster (circa 1370–1450) in the Netherlands in 1440. About 1455, after Coster's death, Johann Gutenberg (circa 1397–1468) printed the first Bible and made Coster's invention famous. Suddenly, the written language was easy to read, cheap, and easy to duplicate. It created one of the major revolutions in the history of the world (Manley 1992, 103).

Historical Note from the Future: The Vikings did not have a printing press—in fact, they did not even know how to read or write. As a result, the rest of the world did not notice the Viking discovery of America circa 1000 C.E. In 1492, after Columbus rediscovered America, the printing press was ready and waiting for him. Within two years after his return, Columbus's description of the New World had been printed into almost every major European language by more than 100 different presses. Due to the printing press, everyone in Europe knew very quickly about Columbus. No one ever heard of Leif Eriksson. The same is true of the Reformation in 1519. Luther's proclamations against the Church in Rome were very quickly printed and spread across modern Germany. Without the printing press, Luther's Reformation of the Church likely would not have succeeded (Boorstin 1983, 510–516).

- Quick Print: Cut thirteen potatoes in half and with the open halves, carve the letters of the alphabet. Cover each of these potato letters with tempera paint and then press them onto a piece of paper forming a letter to a friend.
- Medieval Copyist: One of the major jobs of monks during the Middle Ages was copying Bibles and other religious books by hand. A

time warp suddenly crosses your classroom and everyone in the class is in a monastery during the Middle Ages. There are no printing presses. Everything we want to have must be copied by hand. Every student monk is to be assigned one paragraph (not too long) to be copied in neat printed letters so the people of the next generation can read it. When finished, now imagine copying an entire Bible by candlelight. What did the invention of the printing press do to the written word?

- Poster Power: Create a poster that illustrates the importance of the printing press to world history.
- ADV Imagine: What if the printing press had never been invented? What would our life be like today? What inventions based on the printing press would never have taken place? What would education be like today without the printing press?

4.10.3   Airplanes in the Renaissance

Airplanes are not twentieth-century inventions. Leonardo da Vinci was flying cardboard models of airplanes and helicopters in 1500. Endlessly watching the graceful ravens taking off and landing near his castle window, Leonardo carefully designed and flew cardboard gliders that copied the graceful aerodynamic shapes of ravens' wings. With wind-up screw motors, he also designed and flew the first cardboard helicopters. What he did not design, however, was a means of designing a human-powered airplane. He worked endlessly on plans for a human to fly by flapping his airplane's wings, but it never worked. The Renaissance in which Leonardo lived was still dominated by a very powerful Church that did not like new ideas. As a result, Leonardo wrote all his plans for airplanes and helicopters in mirror writing so that no one would accuse him of witchcraft (Manley 1992, 103).

- Paper Airplane: Make a paper airplane and then measure how far it flies.
- Design Comparison: How many different paper airplane designs are known by members of your class?
- Test Pilot: Test out different paper airplane designs to see which one flies the farthest. Which one can stay in the air the longest? Which one can fly in circles? Which one can fly in loops?

- Aerodynamic Design: Discuss in teams of four and then the whole class the aerodynamics of each paper airplane. What makes each fly and do different tricks? Why does one paper airplane fly farther than the others? Why is one paper airplane design better than the other?
- Bird Watching: Watch the graceful flight of a large bird like a raven or seagull near your home and school, like Leonardo did. What do you notice about the raven's flight that makes it take off and land so easily?
- Raven Drawing: Make a drawing of a raven's wings and tail when it is landing and describe why you think the raven does this.
- Role Play: Imagine you are Leonardo da Vinci (500 years ago) watching ravens in the sky and making the world's first paper airplanes. Describe your discoveries in an essay and then read it to the class.
- ADV Research: Using the resources in your library and on the Internet, examine the basic principles of aerodynamics for modern airplanes and compare them to the fundamental discoveries of Leonardo in 1500.

4.11.0   ART AND CREATIVE THOUGHT

4.11.1   The Father of the Renaissance

Francesco ("Petrarch") Petracco (1304–1375) is acknowledged as one of the fathers of the Renaissance. Writing in exile from Avignon, the native Florentine became the rage of all Italy with his expressions of pure love and the love of nature in the Italian language. He wrote imaginary letters to the great Greek and Roman writers—Homer, Cicero, and Livy. In so doing, he alone revived an interest in the classical world. Rather than extol the virtue of faith in the Church, he cherished the simple personal pleasures of love, watching nature, and even climbing mountains—just for the joy of doing pleasurable things. With Petrarch, suddenly, an individual's feelings, emotions, and pleasures were important. With these concerns for the individual pleasures and not religious doctrine of faith, Petrarch became one of the fathers of the Renaissance (Durant 1953).

- Quick Write: Describe a scene from nature you enjoy and why you enjoy it.

- Quick Poem: Describe this simple natural pleasure of yours in a short poem à la Petrarch.
- Ace Reporter: As the ace reporter for the *Renaissance Times* newspaper, develop a list of questions to ask Petrarch in an interview. With a partner, develop a set of answers you think Petrarch might say to your questions and then present your interview to the class.
- ADV Literary Research: Research your library for something by Petrarch, read it, and then share your impressions of it in class.

4.11.2   England's First Comedy

Geoffrey Chaucer (1340?–1400) wrote a very funny set of poetic stories in English called *Canterbury Tales,* between 1386 and 1399. The Middle Ages were really not a very fun time. There was one exception: religious pilgrimages. These pilgrimages were not really meant to be fun, but people traveling together toward holy sites sang, told funny stories, met interesting people, and basically had a good time. In reality, religious pilgrimages became the tourist industry of the Middle Ages. As did Boccaccio, he wrote one of the first human comedies since the classical period of ancient Greece and Rome. Chaucer's thirty pilgrims were all sorts of people—a knight, a nun, a clerk, a man of law, and a miller's wife. Each told funny tales, each had a moral, and all were quite entertaining. *Canterbury Tales* was one of England's first steps toward the Renaissance.

- Quick Write: Write down a funny story you recently heard, and share it with your class.
- Ad Campaign: Put together an ad campaign to sell *Canterbury Tales* on the open market with an ad poster and a thirty-second TV spot.
- ADV Quick Publish: Compare the stories that members of your class have told. If your collected stories are good enough, print them together and sell them to other students as a class project to earn money for a class party.

4.11.3   Black Plague and Human Comedy—1348

Giovanni Boccaccio (1313–1375) thankfully survived the black plague that struck Florence and killed half of its population in 1348. His famous comedy *Decameron* is based on this attack of the black plague, and with it, Boccaccio became the first writer of the Renaissance. There are no morals or religious teachings in Boccaccio's *Decameron*. These are only one hundred tales told by seven young ladies and three young men who have come together to escape the plague. The stories are of love, courage, cowardice, humor, wisdom, deceit, and foolishness. Boccaccio's tales are the first book in the world of modern short stories. One story is of Ghismunda, who falls in love with her father's valet. The father disapproves of someone so lowly for his daughter and kills his valet. To console his daughter, the father gives her a solid gold goblet containing the valet's heart. In the final scene, she puts poison in the goblet and tells her father: "Will you say I consorted with a man of low condition? Poverty does not diminish anyone's ability, it only diminishes his wealth! Many kings and great rulers were once poor, and many of those who plow the land and watch the sheep were once very rich, and they still are." She then drinks the poison to be reunited with her lover's heart (Boorstin 1992, 266–275).

- Quick Disaster: Imagine you are caught in a major disaster in which thousands of people die. You and your friends seriously think the world is about to come to an end. To take your minds off the disaster, write down several things you would talk about to other surviving friends. Would it be something sad, funny, or serious?
- Ace Reporter: As the ace reporter of the *Renaissance Times* newspaper, give an eyewitness account of the black plague as it hits Florence in 1348. With your editorial team (groups of four students), develop a front-page edition focusing on the plague and people's reactions to it (McNeill 1977).
- Writer's Corner: In Boccaccio's style, write a short story with a twist or two in its plot about love, anger, fear, joy, or lying. Share your short Boccaccio-style story with your class.
- Music Mart: Make up a funny song with a partner about the black plague—something Boccaccio would like—and share it with your class.
- ADV Literary Research: How many great pieces of literature were written in times of crisis? Why does this happen?

4.11.4   Brunelleschi's Dome

Filippo Brunelleschi (1377–1446) and his buddy, the sculptor Donatello (1389?–1466), were fanatics about ancient Rome. They drew and measured almost every ruin they could find in ancient Rome. The result was a Florentine architect who understood and who could, once again, create buildings that paralleled the grandeur of the Pantheon in ancient Rome. Florence had begun their cathedral in 1296, and it was to be the grandest in Europe with a dome 138.5 feet across. The difficulty was that no one since the ancient Romans knew how to build such a large dome. In 1425, Brunelleschi got the final contract to complete the dome with an ingenious trick that is still used by architects today. He used a tall outer dome to give the cathedral height and then a false inner dome, which would look more full to the viewers inside the cathedral. The two domes together strengthened each other and the whole structure. To make the outer dome stronger, he made it into an octagon similar to a Gothic church from the Middle Ages, but it was a true dome and the largest built since ancient Rome, more than 1,200 years before. Brunelleschi's dome in Florence represented the full expression of the Renaissance in Italy—a rebirth of the grandeur of ancient Greece and Rome (see Symcox 1991).

Note from the Future: This same double dome was used in building other giant domes, such as St. Paul's Cathedral in London and the dome of the Capitol Building in Washington, D.C. Both used Brunelleschi's design as a model (Boorstin 1992, 384–391).

- Quick Write: Describe the most impressive building you have ever seen. What made it impressive to you?
- Cheer Leader: Create a Renaissance cheer to encourage Brunelleschi to finish his famous dome.
- Quick Calc: With rulers or a measuring tape, measure 138.5 feet across an area in your school yard. This is the diameter of Brunelleschi's dome in Florence. From this measurement, have all the students in class stand in a circle with this diameter to represent the size of Brunelleschi's dome. Impressive, isn't it?
- Model Mart: Create a cardboard model of the cathedral at Florence and especially Brunelleschi's dome. Describe how you constructed this dome out of cardboard.
- What If?: Imagine being the construction foreman in charge of all the materials (the rock, cement, and brick) used to create Brunelleschi's dome. Describe in a short paragraph or two what a workday of yours would be like.
- ADV Architectural Comparison: Compare the size and shape of some of the great domed buildings in the world—the Parthenon, the Blue Masjid in Istanbul, St. Peter's in Rome, St. Paul's in London,

and the Capitol Building in Washington, D.C. How are they similar and different from each other?

4.11.5   Da Vinci's Revolution in Oil Painting

During the Middle Ages and before, pictures were painted on walls and wood, usually with a mixture of color dye and egg yolk. That all changed radically with the Renaissance. Starting with Jan van Eyck (d. 1441) in the Netherlands, painters started to paint with slow-drying, oil-based paints. These oil-based paints enabled the artist to slowly layer subtle different shades of hue and color to make very realistic skin tones. The oil-based paints were also superior at refracting light, resulting in very bright colors. Two well-known Italian painters quickly became champions of this new way of painting—Leonardo da Vinci and Raphael. One of the first oil paintings by Leonardo is also perhaps the most famous in the world, *La Gianconda* (otherwise known as the *Mona Lisa*). Within one hundred years (by 1550), every major painter of the Renaissance was painting in oils (Manley 1992, 128).

Note from the Future: Until the invention of acrylics in the late twentieth century, virtually every major artist in the world in the past 400 years after the Renaissance used oil as a major way of painting.

- Art Mart: Paint a picture of a person using watercolors.
- Close-Up and Personal: With a set of paintings from the Renaissance in your library or on the Internet, use a magnifying glass to look closely at an oil painting form the Renaissance. Can you see the careful layering of different hues and colors that soften the painting and make it so personal and lifelike? Describe, in a short paragraph, what you see.
- Gallery Walk: Pick out four or five great oil paintings from the Renaissance by Leonardo, Raphael, and others.
  - Which one is the most impressive? Why?
  - Which one is the most realistic? Why?
  - Which one is the most colorful? Why?
  - Which one do you like the best? Why?
- ADV Art Critic: Compare your work of art with a great Renaissance painting, such as the *Mona Lisa*. Describe the differences between the colors and textures of your watercolor and the Renaissance oil painting.
- ADV Art Research: Using resources in your library and on the Internet, describe in an essay what oil painting did for the Renaissance over 400 years ago and what it did for the whole history of painting.

4.11.6   Painting the Ceiling—Ugh!—In 1512

Michelangelo Buonarroti (1475–1564) at age thirty-three did not want to paint the Sistine Chapel ceiling. He was perhaps the greatest sculptor the world had ever seen. He told Pope Julius repeatedly that he did not want to do it. The Pope bullied him, yelled at him, hit him with his cane—and Michelangelo finally agreed to do it. He started painting the 132-by-44-foot ceiling in 1508 and finished it in 1512. He did not enjoy the exhausting experience and described what it felt like: "I live here in great toil and great weariness of body, and have no friends of any kind and don't want any, and haven't the time to eat what I need."

We can pity poor Michelangelo toiling alone, cold and endlessly at the top of the 100-foot scaffolding with the pope continually screaming at him, but the end product is perhaps the greatest painting the world has ever seen—and remains so almost 500 years later (Jeffery 1989, 688–713; Boorstin 1992, 407–419).

- Quick Write: Imagine working alone as a painter for three years on a ceiling 100 feet in the air. Describe your feelings in a short paragraph.
- Poster Power: Create a poster for Pope Julius to hang outside the Vatican to advertise for a painter of the Sistine Chapel in 1508.
- Scaffold Sticker: Create a scaffold sticker for Michelangelo to use to express how he felt as he painted the Sistine Chapel.
- Art Mart: Create a design for painting the ceiling of your classroom and present it to your class.
- Pro or Con: In a pair share, stage a mock argument whether or not Pope Julius was ultimately correct in forcing Michelangelo to work hard on the Sistine Chapel.
- ADV Sistine Tour: Find a large art book illustrating the different sections of the ceiling of the Sistine Chapel. Write down a brief description of each section of the painting and then describe your favorite section to your class.
- ADV Art Research: Using resources in your library and on the Internet, compare Michelangelo's Sistine Chapel with any other major work of art in the world. How do they compare? Report your findings to the class.

4.11.7   Revolt against the Renaissance

Not everyone loved Renaissance art. The old medieval Christian iconoclast idea that painting pictures of humans was evil still existed in

Germany and elsewhere. At several times during the Reformation, Church art was destroyed by iconoclastic Protestant mobs. Most of the destruction of Renaissance art, however, took place in England under the rule of Henry VIII. He joined the Protestant revolt in 1538 against the authority of the pope in Rome, officially to annul his marriage to Catherine of Aragon. Unofficially, however, he wanted to take control of all the Church's wealth in England. By creating his own "Protestant" Church, Henry also took control of all Church property. All gold and silver items were immediately taken by the crown and melted down. Major paintings were smashed, books were burned, altars were destroyed, and stained-glass windows broken. Virtually all Church art in England before 1538 was destroyed by mobs under the direction of Henry VIII (Manley 1992, 128).

- Quick Write: What is your immediate reaction when you see a work of art that has been disfigured or destroyed, such as Michelangelo's *Pieta*?
- Pair Share: In a pair share, discuss for one minute each whether or not people with religious values that oppose certain kinds of art have the right to destroy art they do not like.
- Class Discussion:
  ◦ Do artists have the right to make any kind of art they want?
  ◦ Should certain rules be placed on artists to make only certain kinds of art?
  ◦ What penalties should be placed on people who deface or destroy art?
- Poster Power: Make a poster either supporting or opposing the right of artists to create anything they want.
- Make a Right: In groups of four, make a list of the fundamental rights all artists should have and present this list to the class.
- ADV The Futurist: Explore your library and the Internet for information on groups today that oppose certain types of artwork. What arguments do these groups have against artistic freedom and what position do you take today on this issue? Present your views on the subject to the class.

4.12.0 SUCCESSES AND FAILURES OF THE RENAISSANCE

4.12.1 Success or Failure?

This is the competitive quiz show that challenges teams to list as many reasons as possible why a person, place, or thing is the most important success or failure of the Renaissance, Reformation, and Age of Exploration.

1. Each student team of four draws the name of a Renaissance, Reformation, or Age of Exploration person, place, or thing from a hat.
2. Each team calls out its name and the scorekeeper puts it on the board as the team's name.
3. Using any books or materials available, each student team has fifteen minutes to make as long a list as possible of reasons why that name is the most important of the era.
4. The Renaissance, Reformation, and Age of Exploration names to be used can be as follows or developed from a larger list:

Mona Lisa	the Sistine Chapel	Inquisition
Martin Luther	Giotto	Leonardo da Vinci
Michelangelo	Cheng Ho	Columbus
Magellan	Vasco da Gama	Brunelleschi's dome
Petrarch	Chaucer	Boccaccio
Henry VIII	Pope Leo X	Lorenzo de Medici
Black Plague	Copernicus	Prince Henry of Portugal

5. A scorekeeper will keep track of how many answers each team gives on the board.
6. The team with the most number of "valid" supporting reasons wins a free trip to the library.

4.13.0 MAJOR WORLD PROBLEMS FOR THE RENAISSANCE

4.13.1 How Does a Renaissance in History Start?

The Renaissance was a glorious period in human history—magnificent art was created, important inventions were made, major scientific discoveries were made, and new worlds were discovered. But the question remains, how does such a period get started? What necessary elements come together to produce a chain reaction of creative thinking in art, religion, politics, and discovery? The world today would be a very dreary place if the Renaissance had not taken place.

• Inquiry #1: Ask some friends if they would like to go play baseball or something else fun. Why does a question to start something work sometimes and not work sometimes?

- Inquiry #2: Why do friends start joining in to help with something, but other times you are left to do something all alone?
- ADV Inquiry #3: In teams of four, examine from library readings and interviews the influence of the following factors in making an activity, product, company, or even a country successful.
  1. Key individuals who influence others into new ways of thinking
  2. An environment accepting enough of new ways of thinking
  3. The availability of financial support to new ways of thinking
  4. Sustained and renewed popular and financial support to continually search for new ideas and thinking
- When finished, present your team's findings to the class in the form of a skit, a poster, or a panel discussion.

4.13.2   What Causes a Renaissance in History to End?

Good or bad, every era in history sooner or later comes to an end. The factors that cause a decline vary. Initial conditions that enabled the era, such as economic prosperity, can disappear. The initial energy of the individuals who started an era such as the Renaissance can fade and not be revitalized with new ideas. The era may also be replaced by a more energetic era with newer ideas. All of these factors contributed to the decline of the Italian Renaissance.

Specifically, three major events spelled the end of the Italian Renaissance. The first was political. Although the Italian city-states were unrivaled during the Renaissance for art, their politics remained strictly medieval, with small city-states constantly fighting petty little wars. Machiavelli sought to unify the city-states against their much larger national neighbors—Spain and France—but his calls went unheeded. In 1527, a German Protestant army invaded Catholic Italy and sacked Rome. Three years later, in 1530, Spain formally took control of the Italian city-states (until 1796). The second cause was religious. By 1535, the Protestant Reformation was in full swing in northern Europe and no longer dependent on Rome. The third cause was economic, from multiple fronts. The Protestant Reformation now deprived the Catholic Church in Rome of the rich donations from the new Protestant Churches in Germany. In 1488, the Portuguese had rounded the Cape of Good Hope in Southern Africa on their way to India. By 1502, the Portuguese could sell pepper in Europe at half the price that the merchants in Italy did, due to their cheaper sea route. Suddenly, Italy was no longer the political, religious, and economic power it once was. The

Church, the political power, and the money were no longer there to support the great artists. The Renaissance was over (Durant 1953, 686–723).

- Quick Write: Name a former favorite sports team or musical group that used to be your favorite. What happened to them? Why did they decline? What would they have to do to become a favorite of yours again?
- Chart It: Chart the factors on a time line that led to the decline of the Renaissance in Italy.
- Map Attack: On a blank map of the world, illustrate how the Portuguese, after 1488, were able to obtain cheaper pepper from India than the Italians who had to obtain it from traders traveling along the Silk Road.
- You Were There: Imagine that you were a great artist, Domingo de Siena, in Florence and were supported with the highest salary, the finest apartment, and many rich patrons. Suddenly, it is over. No one has the money to hire you. You are out of work with no apartment and no friends. Describe your feelings in a letter to a friend.
- Poster Power: Make a poster illustrating the three major things that caused the rapid decline of the Renaissance in Italy.
- Historical Analysis: In groups of four, discuss possible ways the Italian city-states could have prevented the decline of the Renaissance. When finished, share your ideas with the class.
- ADV Historical Research: Using resources in the library and on the Internet, examine the decline of several different eras in history and compare their similarities and differences. When finished, report your findings to the class.
- ADV The Futurist: Research the decline of the Renaissance with the decline of a nation or company during the twentieth century. When finished, share your conclusions with the class.

4.14.0   ERA ANTECEDENTS FOR THE FUTURE

4.14.1   Is Humankind Ready to Advance?

It is now time to judge whether or not humankind is ready to advance into the next era. Five members from around the Renaissance Village (the class) will state their basic viewpoints of whether or not enough advances have been made during the Renaissance, and whether humankind should move forward. The five illustrious members are as follows:

1. Letuck de Betrink, the archconservative of Renaissance Village, who believes that humankind has gone far enough with enough progress. Betrink believes strongly that the good old days were the best and that humankind needs to hold strongly to past values and beliefs.
2. Monardo Derudzuk, one of the rising young voices in the town, is a more moderate conservative who believes that we need to be very cautious with any change and be very sure that no harm will come to Renaissance Village if change takes place. Monardo is willing to accept some change, but only in very small amounts and only when the time is right—and wants to decide when that time will come.
3. Peeangelo Wookbot, the wishy-washy middle-of-the-roader around the village, is willing to accept change for a few minutes after one speaker, but might have a change of mind in an instant to oppose change after another speaker has finished.
4. Yakurnicus Vatsmeer, the moderate progressive of the group, is willing to support change for the good of the people in Renaissance Village. Vatsmeer is especially in favor of change that will benefit Vatsmeer's own family directly.
5. Quether Varull, the radical progressive of the village, is very willing to support any change that will move humanity away from the drafty and damp old castle into something more modern and comfortable for humanity.

- Pick a Position: Each member of Renaissance Village (classroom) now must chose one of the five positions for humanity to take and support their position with evidence of what they have learned about the Renaissance.
- Class Vote: A vote will then be taken of all peasants and nobles around town to determine whether or not humanity should move on to the next era. The consensus decision of the imaginary citizens of Renaissance Village will determine their own future and the rest of humanity. (In reality, such decisions by people during the Renaissance were key in deciding whether humans stayed the way they were or progressed to new levels of development.)

Full Thematic Table of Contents

Traditional World History: Chronological and Regional Table of Contents

Basic Map Resources

Absolutely the best source of maps for any world history class is the CD-ROM by Broderbund entitled "Maps N Facts." Any map of any country or continent can be instantly analyzed or printed out for duplication, along with a massive wealth of CIA data on any area of the world. Available from Broderbund, P.O. Box 6125, Novato, CA 94948.

An excellent map source on the Internet is Bruce Jones Designers' World of Maps (see https://www.bjdesign.com), from which you can download excellent sets of maps for both the IBM PC and MAC computers for a low initial price. BJDesign is the source for the beautiful black continental global maps that are contained in this appendix.

The Internet also contains a wealth of other map sources for a wide variety of needs. For example, the library at the University of Texas, Austin, has a large collection of Asian maps available on the Web at http://www.lib.utexas.edu/PCL/Map_collection/asia.html. A West End London bookstore, Altea Maps & Books, sells antique maps online at http://www.antique-maps.co.uk. For a comprehensive site of world maps on the Web, The Map Guide! at http://wwww.algonet.se/~cristar/index.htm lists almost every map available on the Web by continents, countries, and region. Check them out!

Recommended Classroom
Background Music by Time Period

Unit 1—Prehistoric Classroom Background Music

Ancient humans sang music and played instruments such as the drum (hollow log), whistle (hollow reed), and harp (stretched animal intestines), but we do not know what ancient music really sounded like. Members of your class, however, are free to experiment and produce sounds that might have sounded like that of ancient humans.

Perhaps the best example of what early harp music sounded like is *The Art of Harp* from the International Harp Festival, Volume One (Earth Beat CD R272496) available from Earth Beat, P.O. Box 1460, Redway, California 95560. This CD is an awesome collection of harp music from such distant locations as Ireland, Germany, and Uganda.

Unit 2—Ancient Classroom Background Music

Written music does not appear until unit 3 (the Middle Ages), but we do have some idea of what kind of instruments were played from written descriptions from wall paintings of the ancient Egyptians, Greeks, and Romans. Following these models and ancient instruments still used in the Middle East, Ali Jihad Racy has produced an interesting CD entitled *Ancient Egypt* [LYRCD 7347] produced by Lyrichord Discs, 141 Perry St., New York, NY 10014. We really do not know how ancient Egyptian music sounded, but Racy's CD is likely to be as close as we can get to the way it might have sounded.

For ancient Greece, a CD from France is entitled *Musique de la Grece Antique* by the Atrium Musicae de Madrid under the leadership of Gregorio Paniagua [Harmonia Mundi HMA1901015]. The CD gives us a fascinating glimpse of the music of ancient Greece based on the rare fragments of papyrus and marble containing music hymns or comments concerning music. Examples include the "Premier Hymn to Apollo" found on a marble slab at Delphi in 1893 and a "Hymn to the Sun" based on a Byzantine papyrus preserved by Galileo in Venice in 1581.

Unit 3—Medieval Classroom Background Music

The last few years have also seen a renaissance of recordings of music from the Middle Ages. Most impressive is the four-CD set entitled The Medieval Experience [Archiv Production 449 082 2 by Deutsche Grammophon] containing Gregorian chants, songs of troubadours, motets, and masses from the Middle Ages and played and sung by such distinguished groups as the Early Music Consort of London and the choir of the monks of the abbey of Notre Dame de Fontgombault. Also impressive are recent CDs celebrating the Jewish, Christian, and Muslim multicultural contributions to the medieval music of Spain. Iberian Garden [Dorian Discovery DIS 80151] by the Altramar Medieval Music Ensemble contains fascinating medieval selections from all three religious groups. More specific is Musique Arabo-Andalouse [Harmonia Mundi CD 90389] by the Atrium Muisicae de Madrid. The sheer elegance and beauty of Muslim culture in Andalucia [Al Andalus] is captured musically in this recreation of the music of Muslim Spain during the Middle Ages, based on the musical traditions of the descendants of Muslim Andalusians still living in Morocco.

Unit 4—Renaissance Classroom Background Music

A wide variety of CDs exist that reconstruct the music of the era of the Renaissance and Explorations. *Canzoni e Danze* [Deutsche Grammophon Archiv Production D111360] by Piffaro: the Renaissance Band creates a delightful wind ensemble of canzoni and dances played on such archaic instruments as bagpipes, shawns, sagbuts, recorders, crumhorns, and harps. *A Song of David: the Music of the Sephardim and Renaissance Spain* [Dorian Discovery DIS 80130] played by La Rondinella reconstructs Jewish Ladino Sephardic music of Spain before their expulsion in 1492 and still preserved by the Jewish Ladino communities in the Balkans. *1492—Music from the Age of Discovery*

[EMI Classics D115591] by the Waverly Consort presents a fascinating selection of songs such as a praise to Fernando [King Ferdinand] for conquering the Moors; a sad love song of three Moorish girls; and an Arabic Andalusian instrumental piece; and selections from the palace song book of the Duke of Alba.

Recommended CD-ROMs and Web Sites by Time Period

Unit 1—Prehistoric CD-ROMs and Web Sites

One of the best classroom CD-ROMs available on early humans and prehumans is *Investigating Olduvai—Archaeology of Human Origins* by Jeanne Sept and produced by the Indiana University Press at www.indiana.edu/iupress or 1-800-842-6796. Through interactive detective work, students learn archaeological field principles, early human prehistory, and early African archaeology. Updates on the Olduvai CD-ROM can also be obtained from the same Web site.

For a real hands-on study of human prehistory, half-scale and full-scale replicas of human, prehuman, and primate skulls (such as *H. erectus*, *H. Neanderthal*, and *A.Afarensis*) can be obtained from Ants in Albuquerque, New Mexico at www.ants-inc.com or 1-800-842-5275. With 3-D glasses, students can also see and study these prehuman replicas free of charge on the Ants Web site.

Unit 2—Ancient CD-ROMs and Web Sites

Thousands of Web sites focus on ancient history. A few of the better ones are as follows:

Ancient Egypt Resources at www.trms.ga.net/~jtucker/lessons/ss/egypt_ancient.html contains a wide list of links to almost any topic on classical Egypt from mummies and Nefertiti to ancient Egyptian medicines and writing your name in hieroglyphics.

Ancient Civilizations on the Internet at www.eliz.tased.edu.au/ancient.htm contains major links to Web sites on ancient Egypt,

Greece, Rome, and even sites on such topics as the Dead Sea Scrolls and ancient Roman cooking.

Exploring Ancient World Cultures at http://eawc.evansville.edu/ provides a discussion of all the major classical civilizations of the world—China, India, the Middle East, as well as Egypt, Greece, and Rome, with hyperlinks to other sites.

Unit 3—Medieval CD-ROMs and Web Sites

Argos–Limited Area Search of the Ancient and Medieval Internet at http://aros.evansville.edu/index.htm is an excellent starting ground for any study of the Middle Ages with hyperlink jumps to sites on the Byzantine Empire, The Labyrinth (a World Wide Web server for medieval studies), and women and gender issues during the Middle Ages. Voted as one of the best sites on Islam by many sources, http://www.mosque.com is a rich multimedia source on the religion of Muhammad.

Unit 4—Renaissance CD-ROMs and Web Sites

Three notable CD-ROMs exist on the Renaissance era: *Leonardo the Inventor* (CD-ROM 37 0072 00); *Explorers of the New World* (CD-ROM 0069 0150 00 by Future Vision Multimedia of Great Neck, New York. Telephone: 516-773-0990); and *Uffizi—A Virtual Tour* (Lifestyle Software Group. Telephone 904-794-7070), an absolutely beautifully designed CD-ROM guiding the viewer carefully through the world's oldest art gallery.

Several outstanding Web sites on the Internet also exist on the era: The Renaissance Web site http://renaissance.dm.net/compendium/home.html offers a delightful *Compendium of Common Knowledge* of the Elizabethan era in England 1558–1603 for writers, actors, and reenactors of such items as games, money, food, language, nobility, and dueling. Welcome to the Renaissance Faire at http://renfaire.com is a how-to-do-it manual for Renaissance Faires, from costumes and language to historical perspectives, and links to California Renaissance Faire sites for specific advise. On the Reformation, the best place to start is http://infoseek.com/topic/education/history/reformation, which leads to a variety of educational sites on the Reformation, including a usefulness ranking and a teachers' chat room on the Reformation. For advanced research on the Reformation, The Protestant Reformation at http://history.hanover.edu/early/prot.htm provides links to approximately forty of the major authors and texts on the Reformation. The Columbus Navigation Homepage at http://www1.minn.net/~keithp/index.htm also provides an interesting site focused on the history, navigation, and specific voyages of Columbus.

Annotated Bibliography

Abercrombie, Thomas J. 1988. When the Moors Ruled Spain. *National Geographic* 174 (July): 86–119.
A beautiful illustrated depiction of the Muslim history of Spain.

———. 1991. Ibn Batutta—Prince of Travelers. *National Geographic* 180 (December): 2–49.
A beautifully told and photographed record of Ibn Batutta's fourteenth-century travels.

Ajayi, J. F. Ade, and Ian Espie. 1965. *A Thousand Years of West African History*. Ibadan (Nigeria): Ibadan University Press.
A classic and masterful source for information on West African history.

Assmann, Ian. 1997. *Moses the Egyptian*. Cambridge, Mass.: Harvard University Press.
A powerful reexamination of the role of Moses in the development of monotheism.

Barreto, Mascarenhas. 1992. *The Portuguese Columbus—Secret Agent of King John II*, translated by Reginald A. Brown. New York: St. Martin's Press.
If you think history is boring, try reading Barreto. This work by Professor Barreto is a report on a lifelong focus on the evidence and validity of the evidence about the man we call Columbus. It turns the conventional wisdom about Columbus upside down.

Boorstin, Daniel J. 1994. *Cleopatra's Nose—Essays on the Unexpected*. New York: Random House.

———. 1992. *The Creators: A History of the Heroes of Imagination*. New York: Random House.

———. 1983. *The Discoverers*. New York: Random House.
Without question, the best book on the discoveries of humankind—social, political, scientific, and just sheer adventure—is this volume by Boorstin. It should be required reading for every student of history.

Bromer, Jeff. 1988. Joan of Arc Rides to the Rescue of New Orleans. *Old News* (November): 1–5.
Old News is a great and inexpensive resource for history teachers and can be obtained for them at 400 Stackstown Road, Marietta, PA 17647 or by phoning 717-426-2212.

Bronowski, J. 1973. *The Ascent of Man*. Boston: Little, Brown.
A beautiful and brilliant history of the human intellect.

Canby, Cortland. 1961. *Epic of Man*. New York: Time, Inc.
A magnificently illustrated coffee table book on the rise of human history.

Capra, Fritjof. 1996. *The Web of Life*. New York: Anchor Books.
A brilliant synthesis of recent thinking tying together the ideas of complexity, Gaia, and chaos theory with explanations of living organisms, ecosystems and social systems.

Carey, John, ed. 1987. *Eyewitness to History*. New York: Avon.
Perhaps one of the most extensive collections of firsthand historical accounts of major events in world history.

Chadwick, John. 1958. *The Decipherment of Linear B*. Cambridge: Cambridge University Press.
A fascinating and detailed account of how the ancient Linear B writing of ancient Greece was decoded.

Chambers, E. K. 1930. *William Shakespeare*. Oxford: Oxford University Press.
A classic source on information about the Elizabethan bard.

Collingwood, R. G. 1956. *The Idea of History*. New York: Galaxy.
A classic source on the philosophy of history.

Confucius. 1971. *Confucian Analects: The Great Learning and the Doctrine of the Mean*. New York: Dover.
This small book captures the essence of Confucian thought.

Dubos, Rene. 1974. *Beast or Angel? Choices That Make Us Human*. New York: Scribner.
A fundamental book for the beginning of human history focusing on a discussion that should take place at the start of every class in history.

Durant, Will. 1939. *The Life of Greece*. New York: Simon & Schuster.

——. 1944. *Caesar and Christ*. New York: Simon & Schuster.

——. 1950. *The Age of Faith*. New York: Simon & Schuster.

——. 1953. *The Renaissance*. New York: Simon & Schuster.

——. 1954. *Our Oriental Heritage*. New York: Simon & Schuster.
The first part of Durant's monumental eight-volume history of the world. Readable, insightful, and always one of the best general references for world history up to the nineteenth century.

———. (1957). *The Reformation*. New York: Simon & Schuster.

Ebrey, Patricia E. 1991. *Chinese Civilization and Society*. New York: Free Press.
A book of social and political historical sources on Chinese history.

Edwards, Mike. 1996. Lord of the Mongols: Genghis Khan. *National Geographic* 190 (December): 2–37.
An excellent short history of the Mongols and their infamous leader Genghis Khan with the usual magnificent photographs, illustrations, and maps of the National Geographic Society.

Eisenman, Robert. 1997. *James—The Brother of Jesus*. New York: Penguin.
A powerful academic inquiry into the early history of Christianity focusing on the leadership of James in Jerusalem between 30 C.E. and 69 C.E. and using such sources as the Dead Sea Scrolls.

Ellwood, Robert S., Jr. 1980. *An Invitation to Japanese Civilization*. Belmont, Calif.: Wadsworth.
A short and lively introduction to the social and intellectual history of Japan.

Fletcher, Sir Banister. 1896. *A History of Architecture on the Comparative Method*. London: B.T. Batsford.
A beautiful old book full of architectural drawings of some of the great buildings of the world.

Gabrieli, Francisco. 1957. *Arab Historians of the Crusades*. New York: Dorset Press.
Perhaps the only readily available Muslim source of firsthand accounts of the Crusades.

Grant, Michael. 1964. *The Birth of Western Civilization—Greece and Rome*. New York: McGraw-Hill.
One of the best of the many magnificently illustrated books on ancient Greece and Rome.

Guedj, Denis. 1996. *Numbers: The Universal Language*. New York: Abrahms.
A beautiful and very readable history of numbers and mathematics.

Gumus, Dogan. 1994. *Ancient Ephesus*. Istanbul: DO-GU Yayinlari.
A beautifully illustrated guidebook to ruins of the ancient Greek and Roman city of Ephesus in southwestern Turkey.

Healey, John F. 1990. *Reading the Past: The Early Alphabet*. Berkeley: University of California Press.
A short, very easily read book on the early forms of modern writing.

Hesse, Hermann. 1951. *Siddhartha*. New York: New Directions Paperbacks.
Perhaps the best short and easy-to-read introduction to the life of the Buddha (Siddhartha).

Jacobus, Lee A., ed. 1994. *The World of Ideas*. Boston: St. Martin's.

Jean, Georges. 1992. *Writing: The Story of Alphabets and Scripts*. New York: Abrahms.
A fun and beautifully edited book, good enough to just look at the pictures and all the different scripts of the world—if not in the mood to read.

Jeffery, David. 1989. A Renaissance for Michelangelo. *National Geographic* 176 (December) 688–713.
A visual treat of the restoration of Michelangelo's ceiling of the Sistine Chapel in the Vatican.

Josephus, Flavius. 1988. *Josephus: The Essential Writings,* translated by Paul L. Maier. Grand Rapids, Mich.: Kregel Publications.
The primary source document for the history of the Jewish people during the early years of the current era and likely a major source of information for early Christian writers such as Luke.

Kennedy, Paul. 1987. *The Rise and Fall of the Great Powers*. New York: Random House.
A powerful study of the cycles of political states.

Koning, Hans. 1991. *Columbus: His Enterprise—Exploding the Myth*. New York: Monthly Review Press.
A critical but very readable investigation into the myths about Columbus and the brutality of the Spaniards against the people of the Caribbean. Not a very pretty picture of our "hero" Columbus.

Kuiseko, Ryokushu. 1988. *Brush Writing—Calligraphy for Beginners*. Tokyo (Japan): Kodansha International.
An excellent step-by-step guide to Japanese calligraphy.

Kunzig, Robert. 1997. The Face of an Ancestral Child. *Discover* 18 (December): 88–101.
A valuable update on the latest excavations of early human archaeological sites from the past one million years.

Manley, Deborah. 1992. *The Guinness Book of Records—1492*. New York: Facts on File.
Simply one of the most interesting books in print. Each page is full of economic, social, political, and geographic information about the year 1492.

McNeil, William H. 1977. *Plagues and People*. New York: Anchor Doubleday.
The classic source for information on the black plague and other epidemics.

Mee, Charles L., Jr. 1993. *Playing God—Seven Fateful Moments When Great Men Met to Change the World*. New York: Simon & Schuster.
An excellent source on the meeting between Attila and Pope Leo I, Cortez and Montezuma, and the meetings at Versailles and Yalta following World Wars I and II.

Meskill, John. 1965. *The Pattern of Chinese History*. Boston: D. C. Heath.

An excellent short source for the major problems confronting Chinese history (for example, cycles, development, or stagnation). One of Heath's series of Problems in Asian Civilizations.

Michael, Franz. 1986. *China through the Ages*. Boulder, Colo.: Westview Press.
An interesting high-level history of the major trends in Chinese history.

Pahl, Ron H. 1997. Maybe Shakespeare Was Right about "Race." *Multicultural Education* (spring): 12–17.
An important article on the historical evolution of the word "race" in the English language.

Pearson, Carol S. 1989. *The Hero Within: Archetypes We Live By*. San Francisco: Harper and Row.
A masterpiece of understanding the role that myths and archetypes play in shaping the lives of individual humans and nations.

Pellegrino, Charles. 1993. *Unearthing Atlantis—An Archaeological Odyssey*. New York: Vintage.
A must-read for anyone interested in the early history of the Mediterranean. Focused on the gigantic volcanic eruption on the Greek Island of Thera (1628 B.C.E.), Pellegrino's look weaves the implications of this eruption on the history of the whole area. Fascinating.

Sardar, Zuauddin, and Zafar Abbas Malik. 1994. *Introducing Muhammad*. New York: Totem Books.
A delightful, beginning introduction to Muhammad and Islam written in a well-illustrated, semi-cartoon format.

Severy, Merle. 1983. The Byzantine Empire—Rome of the East. *National Geographic* 164 (December): 709–736, 746–766.
A beautiful journey with the Byzantines in the best National Geographic *tradition.*

Shenkman, Richard. 1993. *Legends, Lies and Cherished Myths of World History*. New York: HarperCollins.
A delightful romp through history, exposing many cherished beliefs as frauds or at least rather rich embellishments.

Shlain, Leonard. 1999. *The Alphabet versus the Goddess—The Conflict between Word and Image*. New York: Penguin.
A brilliant study of the mental differences between male and female, and the negative impact illiteracy has had on females throughout history.

Sussman, Robert W. 1997. Exploring Our Basic Human Nature: Are Humans Inherently Violent? *Anthro Notes* 19 (fall): 1–6, 17–19.
A great starting point for any thoughtful class on the history of humanity.

Symcox, Linda. 1991. *Crowning the Cathedral of Florence: Brunelleschi Builds His Dome*. Los Angeles, Calif.: UCLA National Center for History in the Schools.

An excellent short monograph on the rediscovery of dome construction during the Renaissance.

Tschanz, Edmund. 1997. The Arab Roots of European Medicine. *Aramco World* 48 (May/June): 20–31.

Tsu, Lao. 1972. *Tao Te Ching.* Translated by Gia-Fu Feng and Jane English. New York: Vintage.
This edition of the Tao Te Ching *cannot be any more beautiful. A dual Chinese-English edition with photography and layout that captures the essence of the Tao.*

Ulrich, Robert. 1971. *Progress or Disaster? From the Bourgeois to the World Civilization.* New York: New York University Press.

Watson, Francis. 1974. *A Concise History of India.* London: Hames and Hudson.
A well-written and illustrated history of India from the Aryan invasions to rule of Indira Gandhi.

Wilson, Cleveland. 1975. *The Living Socrates.* Owings Mills, Md.: Stemmer House.
A clear and simple application of Socrates to modern living.

Wood, Francis. 1996. *Did Marco Polo Go to China?* Boulder, Colo.: Westview Press.
A scholarly study of the story of Marco Polo that questions whether or not it is true.

About the Author

Ron Pahl is a longtime world history buff who does not like history teachers who bore their students. He has climbed the pyramids of Giza several times, sat with his feet in the reflecting pool of the Taj Mahal, and meditated with monks at Ankhor Wat. Why can't students actively simulate such exciting historical experiences in the classroom? His belief is that students learn more in active, rigorous, and enjoyable classrooms and he has applied this belief to his high school classrooms for more than twenty years. He currently teaches and coordinates the social studies teacher education program at California State University, Fullerton.